Democracy
and Its
Crisis

Other books by the same author

ACADEMIC
An Introduction to Philosophical Logic
The Refutation of Scepticism
Berkeley: The Central Arguments
Wittgenstein
Russell
Philosophy 1: A Guide through the Subject (editor)
Philosophy 2: Further through the Subject (editor)
The Continuum Encyclopedia of British Philosophy (editor)
Truth, Meaning and Realism
Scepticism and the Possibility of Knowledge

GENERAL
The Long March to the Fourth of June (with Xu You Yu)
China: A Literary Companion (with Susan Whitfield)
The Future of Moral Values
The Quarrel of the Age: The Life and Times of William Hazlitt
Herrick: Lyrics of Love and Desire (editor)
What Is Good?
Descartes: The Life and Times of a Genius
Among the Dead Cities
Against All Gods
Towards the Light
The Choice of Hercules
Ideas that Matter
To Set Prometheus Free
Liberty in the Age of Terror
The Good Book
The God Argument
A Handbook of Humanism (editor, with Andrew Copson)
Friendship
The Age of Genius
War

ESSAY COLLECTIONS
The Meaning of Things
The Reason of Things
The Mystery of Things
The Heart of Things
The Form of Things
Thinking of Answers
The Challenge of Things

Democracy
and Its
Crisis

A. C.
GRAYLING

ONEWORLD

A Oneworld Book

First published by Oneworld Publications, 2017

Copyright © A. C. Grayling 2017

The moral right of A. C. Grayling to be identified as the Author of this work has been asserted by him in accordance with the Copyright, Designs, and Patents Act 1988

ISBN 978-1-78607-289-4
eISBN 978-1-78607-290-0

Typeset by Hewer Text UK Ltd
Printed and bound in Great Britain by Clays Ltd, St Ives plc

Oneworld Publications
10 Bloomsbury Street
London WC1B 3SR
England

Stay up to date with the latest books, special offers, and exclusive content from Oneworld with our monthly newsletter

Sign up on our website
oneworld-publications.com

FSC
www.fsc.org
MIX
Paper from
responsible sources
FSC® C018072

To Bill Swainson
philosophus, consuasor, amicus

CONTENTS

PREFACE

This book is about the failure of the best political system we have: democracy. And it is about how to put it right.

'Democracy' has been given many meanings, and the word 'democratic' has even been used to describe political systems that are anything but democratic, those typically known as 'The People's Democratic Republic of X'. But one system of democracy – *representative democracy* – was painstakingly thought out and constructed with the aim of making democracy really work, and was applied in almost all of what we think of as the 'liberal democracies of the Western world'. But in at least two of its leading examples in today's world, the United States and the United Kingdom, representative democracy has been made to fail. Notice these words: 'made to fail'. I argue that if the ideas that underlie the concept of representative democracy were properly and transparently applied, democracy would truly be, as Winston Churchill claimed, the least bad of all systems. But it has been made to fail by a combination of causes, all of them deliberate.

In the pages that follow I explain how the idea of *representative* democracy emerged from a long debate about how to make democracy work (Part I), then discuss what has gone wrong with it in the US and the UK (Part II Chapters 7 and 8) and how to put it right (Part II Chapters 9 and 10). To get a really clear idea of what *representative democracy* is one must understand the process by which the idea of it emerged. If one does not understand the logic of it, one will not understand why it is as it is, and how those who are undermining it are managing to do so.

This is because representative democracy is a structure designed to base sound and stable government on the democratic consent or will of the people. 'Consent', 'will', 'the people', and the way that sound government is to be based on them, are the key contested concepts here, and it is only by understanding how they have been given meaning and effect that we can see what representative democracy is, and what is happening to it. That is why I begin with an account of how the idea of it emerged. (Those not interested in the history and theory of the matter can however go straight to Part II.)

An analogy which, if kept in mind throughout, makes the intention of representative democracy clear, is this: the Australian poet Peter Porter once said, speaking of literature, that 'the purpose of form is to prevent you from putting down on paper the first thing that comes into your head'. Representative democracy is about the *form* of a political order as the vehicle for carrying democratically expressed preferences into good government for all.

In at least two major representative democracies, that vehicle has been seriously tampered with, and among the worst symptoms of this so far to appear are the phenomena of the Trump election in the US and 'Brexit' in the UK.

A. C. Grayling
London, June 2017

INTRODUCTION

For many centuries the idea of democracy was regarded with revulsion and fear, and not just by ruling elites who saw it as against their interests. This prevented the mass of people from having any say in the government of their communities and their own lives. It took much time, ingenuity and careful thought to devise institutions and practices which would make the democratic expression of preferences translatable into government that worked.

For most of recorded history political power has been held by the few over the many. It is easy to imagine that in prehistoric conditions, in small bands of people, an instinctive democracy reigned; but it is equally easy to imagine that a strong individual, charismatic or physically powerful or both, exerted leadership rather as alpha individuals do in other animal species – usually males, which suggests that physical strength had much to do with it. Physical strength is one form of power, but so also are wealth, tradition, mystique, taboo, religious attitudes, genealogy – all in their own ways, and more potently still in combination, providing and justifying the rule of one or a few over the rest.

At different points in history this form of political structure has been challenged and, less frequently, replaced by the claim of the many to have more right than the few to hold political power, or – in terms both more practical and accurate – to be its source. In fifth century BCE Athens this claim took its fundamental form, which is democracy. The word itself originates in the ancient Greek *demokratia*, from *demos* 'the people', *kratos* 'rule': 'rule by the people'. We would not now recognize Athenian democracy as a paradigm, for in effect it was the replacement of a smaller 'few' by a larger 'few'. The franchise was held by adult male citizens only, a minority in the city, excluding women, slaves and *xenoi* (non-citizens), groups which between them probably made up at least three-quarters of the city's adult population.

But Athenian democracy was enough to alarm some of its leading contemporary thinkers, notably Plato, who saw the danger in it: that it could too readily degenerate into what is called *ochlocracy*, that is, mob rule, driven in unruly fashion by emotion, self-interest, prejudice, anger, ignorance and thoughtlessness into rash, cruel, destructive and self-destructive action. The danger is even more apparent when one considers the power of demagoguery, of manipulation of crowd sentiment by fiery rabble-rousing speeches (or their later forms such as, for example, tendentious election advertising) which target those very things – emotion and prejudice – so inimical to producing sound government. This danger is in reality different from ochlocracy, for this is manipulation by a hidden oligarchy – a group using the excuse or the fig-leaf of appeals to democratic licence to carry out their agenda.

The Platonic anxiety about democracy has resonated throughout history. The remark attributed to Winston Churchill as his second comment on democracy (the first being well known: that 'democracy is the worst form of Government except for all those other forms that have been tried from time to time')[1] could be a summary of Plato's own view: that 'the strongest argument against democracy is a few minutes' conversation with any voter', the point being that it reveals the ignorance, self-interest, short-termism and prejudice typical of too many voters. The American satirist H. L. Mencken put the point more trenchantly: 'Democracy is a pathetic belief in the collective wisdom of individual ignorance.'

Of course these cynical views miss the point, and perhaps deliberately so, which the ideal of democracy reaches for. Yet at the same time, in the powerfully justifiable claim of the many to be the holders or source of political authority, and in the danger of the collapse of this authority into either ochlocracy or hidden oligarchy, lies the acute dilemma of democracy itself. Until the seventeenth century scarcely any thought was given to how democracy might be made possible by means of institutions and practices that would honour the right of the many to be the source of political and governmental authority in their society, while securing that arrangement against the danger of ochlocracy or hidden oligarchy. How – this was and remains the burning question – is this to be done?

To appreciate the importance of the question, one need only reflect that if the practical sense as well as the self-interest of most polities in recorded history seems to have been that of two kinds of tyranny – rule by a dictator or a dictatorial claque, and rule by a mob – the former is, unhappily and unavoidably, preferable for reasons too obvious for its proponents to enumerate. Indeed in the opinion of those such as Plato, monarchy and open oligarchy (respectively rule by one and by a few) are less likely to degenerate into tyranny than is democracy, because monarchs and oligarchs would see that their tenure of power relies at least in part on the implicit acceptance of their rule by the populace, which cannot be secured by the exercise of coercive power alone. Hence come the pomp and circumstance, bread and circuses, invocations of divine approval, appeals to tradition, and all the usual trappings by which such rulers sought and in places still seek to awe, inspire or otherwise attach the loyalty or at least the subjection of their people.[2]

For Plato the *demos*, by contrast, a numerous body without a head, is too vulnerable to being captured by the emotion of the moment, by the phenomenon of the 'madness of crowds' which panic or anger can prompt, or which demagogues are by definition skilled at arousing and exploiting.[3]

What Plato did not consider was whether there are ways of so structuring the application of popular consent to the administration of government that the benefits of democracy can be harnessed without risk of it collapsing into either mob rule or tyranny. This work, of considering and then constructing practical means to this end, only fully began with the devisers of the US Constitution in the late eighteenth century. Of course the ideas at stake in this work were not new: the Levellers of seventeenth-century England had eloquently made the case for a form of democracy with universal male suffrage, and their disputants in the Putney Debates of 1647 made an alternative case for a more restricted because more conditional property-based franchise. The latter indirectly issued in the claim in the English Bill of Rights of 1688 that 'the Lords Spiritual and Temporal and Commons' (with the Crown jointly constituting Parliament) 'represent the people' – although the England of 1688 was considerably less a democracy even than Henry Ireton and Oliver Cromwell had envisaged at Putney.

But it was Thomas Jefferson, James Madison and their colleagues in revolutionary America, and in Europe Benjamin

Constant, Alexis de Tocqueville and John Stuart Mill, who formulated ideas of democracy which influenced practical historical events leading to the emergence of increasingly democratic constitutions. A common theme both of the theory and the practice was that the dilemma of democracy could be resolved by so arranging the institutions and practices of the political state that they could reconcile two key aims: that the ultimate source of political authority should lie in democratic assent, and that government should be and could be sound and responsible.

What emerged in practical terms from these considerations was the realization that democracy, in whatever form, is only part of what would make for sound government, though it is obviously a very important and indeed necessary part. But herein lies a key: democracy is necessary, but not by itself sufficient. More is needed, both in the way of further necessities, and of desiderata. Necessities are: constitutional checks and balances placing limits on the power of both legislature and executive, and providing remedies when the limits are breached. Desiderata are: an informed and reflective electorate, and a responsible Fourth Estate as a vehicle for distributing that information and providing a platform for debate and analysis.[4] The briefest of surveys shows by how much the major democracies fell short in respect of both the necessities and the desiderata – and the years 2016–17 demonstrate how that underachievement led to a breakdown of the compromise offered as a solution to the dilemma of democracy.

The argument in what follows, therefore, is this: the political history of what we can call the 'Western liberal democracies' is the history of the development and application of a compromise which resolves democracy's dilemma. To understand the compromise one must know that history. In this book I explore how the compromise emerged and evaluate it, explore the manner and some main causes of its recent breakdown in two polities – the United Kingdom and the United States – and suggest remedies; for, to repeat, it is in my view unarguably right that the model of democracy forged by this compromise is by quite a long way the least bad of a lot of bad systems, and we do well to preserve it if we can.

As regards the two polities on which the following focuses, the reasons for examining how the phenomena of the election of President Donald Trump in the US, and the 'Brexit' referendum and what followed it in the UK, speak for themselves. Granting the presence of other significant causal factors, they most acutely illustrate what happens when there is a failure to cleave to the underlying principles of representative democracy. Were there space to do so, and were this intended as a comprehensive treatise on democracy in general, it would be instructive to examine how the political orders of the French Fifth Republic, the German federal order, and the parliamentary systems of Australia, New Zealand, India and elsewhere which inherited features of the British system fare in the light both of the pressures under which democracy exists – manipulation of electorates by interests employing big money, 'Big Data', hacking, partisan press controlled by powerful and wealthy non-citizens, and the like – and the temporizing that pushes systems away from the principles of representative democracy on which all are theoretically founded to a lesser or greater degree. Throughout what follows readers are invited to remember the various ways in which the underlying principles have been put into effect, and to contemplate how those principles have governed such developments as the 1949 Basic Law of Germany and the constitution of the Fifth Republic in France. Both the UK and US systems are much older and more continuous in their history; in their different ways they illustrate the emergence and application of ideas designed to resolve the dilemma of democracy, which these younger democracies benefited from. This too is a reason for focusing mainly on the US and the UK here.

It would be less instructive to look at Turkey and Russia, which, although they have popular elections, lack the features of representative democracy because the power in the hands of the executive in each case – Turkey, at time of writing, changing its constitution to concentrate yet more power in presidential hands; Russia virtually a tsardom anyway – is effectively unrestricted by weak and functionally cosmetic institutions of democracy, rather like China where much theatre is made of a national 'people's congress' which is wholly without influence on the executive. I mention these examples only in order to set them aside.

There are more reasons than just the obvious ones why defending the underlying principles of representative democracy matters, and I explain and argue for those too, in three related theses. One is that a major part of the problem with politics is politics itself, and that the place of the political in the life of a state or national community needs to be reconfigured. The other is the need for compulsory civic education in schools, and compulsory voting, with qualification for the vote starting at sixteen years of age. The reasons are unarguable, and are discussed later in this book. The third is that in numerous, diverse and complex pluralistic societies the task of managing competing needs and demands is a negotiation, a negotiation that a society has with itself partly through its political processes; and that the solution to the dilemma of democracy discussed in what follows is by some distance the least bad way of doing this. Together the argument is for both a reconfiguration and a restitution of the political order in line with the compromise that the great historical debate about democracy (described in the next chapters) worked out, as an answer to the present risks faced by the institutions and practices of representative democracy when not managed with transparency, clarity, responsibility, and engagement.

The word 'democracy' denotes a number of different political systems, some of them anything but democratic in any meaningful sense of the term; for a speaking example, the official designation of North Korea is 'the Democratic People's Republic of Korea'. The democracy-allusive idea that 'the people' are in control of their country's government and politics – in some sense of 'the people' and some sense of 'control': these are precisely matters to be explored in this book – is claimed by such designations as 'the People's Republic of China'. This formulation was a commonplace of nomenclature for pre-1989 communist regimes; the People's Republics of Poland, Bulgaria, Hungary and Mongolia all dropped the democracy-allusive word 'people' after 1989 in remodelling themselves on the multiparty electoral and parliamentary systems of the Western liberal democracies. The implication is that the formula was an example of Orwellian Newspeak merely, denoting the opposite of reality.

Whatever the history of regimes to which the word 'democratic' has been applied, the clear intention embodied in the idea of democracy is that it is a political order in which government is chosen and given its authority by the periodically, freely and fairly cast votes of the enfranchised members of the populace, who have a real choice as to whom to give their vote. In modern democracies the franchise is extended as widely as is consistent with decisions about who should have and who should be denied a vote, and on what grounds; such decisions include questions about a suitable minimum voting age. Until a century ago qualification for the franchise included how much property a person owned and that person's sex. The idea behind the property qualification was that the vote should be reserved to those with a palpable stake in the state and its economy; the idea behind the sex qualification was that only men were likely to be sufficiently informed and rational to know how to use a vote properly. Needless to say, abolition of these qualifications could not have come soon enough.

The principle underlying democracy thus understood is that it gives the enfranchised an important say in the running of their society, through mechanisms which allow for peaceful changes of government. A central feature of a democratic order is the rule of law, and correlatively the idea that the law applies equally to all and its remedies are equally available to all.[5] Due process is key, protecting against the arbitrary application or withholding of legal provisions. But this is not the only central feature. A set of civil liberties is essential to the operation of democracy, such as freedom of expression, the right to assembly, and liberty in respect of political choices. The mechanisms by which the enfranchised elect a government, and by which the government is thereafter constrained in what it can do, are highly important. Each vote should have equal weight (a condition not satisfied by a first-past-the-post electoral system: see pp. 138–42), and there should be clear constitutional provisions governing the exercise of governmental power and discretion (in the UK there is insufficient such clarity because the constitution is unwritten and consists in an inchoate mixture of custom and statute).

All this is essential to democracy. Is it enough? Not yet. Three further intimately connected essentials – the proper operation of the democracy, the quality of the electorate, and the quality of the elected – would close the gap between aspiration and the nearest thing to the ideal that humanity can achieve in this sphere. I shall suggest that it is in the breakdown of these further essentials that the crisis of contemporary democracy consists.

In the first half of the book I set out the background to the dilemma of democracy and the solutions proposed for the dilemma. I start with the reasons for opposition to the idea of democracy which, for over two thousand years, deprived people almost everywhere of a voice in the government of their lives (chapters 1–2); and then trace the debates which led to a solution to the dilemma and the promise of a workable democracy (chapters 3–6). Much scholarship and debate surround the work of each of the thinkers I discuss; I go to their original arguments themselves to show how each made his (all 'his' as it happens) case.

A knowledge of these matters is essential to grasping what is, can and should be understood about the important concept of democracy, so that the next steps – understanding what has gone wrong with democracy in leading parts of the Western world, and what can be done to reclaim the solution so painfully and at such length worked out by the long tradition of debate about it – can be better done (chapters 7–10).

This story shows that democracy as one of the leading principles of the contemporary advanced world has to be the most discussed, thought about and thought out feature of our social and political arrangements. Allowing it to be corroded, as it has been, is a serious dereliction of our duty as citizens. I describe our forebears' long and arduous struggle to achieve the rights and liberties founded on democracy in my *Towards the Light* (2011); allowing democracy to be corrupted as it has been is a betrayal of that struggle, and a danger to our present and our future.

This last apocalyptic-seeming remark is offered in all sober-ness. It is very easy to lose what is of real value by inattention, laziness, the sloppiness induced by overconfidence and distraction by trivia. While we look at the screens of our televisions and mobile phones, others with agendas have their fingers in the pockets of our democracy, on the steering wheel of our democracy, on the keys to our democracy, on the credit cards of our democracy. As I write this in the spring of 2017, and as a motivation for writing it, I take it to be the case that the United Kingdom is in the throes of a politically illegitimate effort – the so-called 'Brexit' – by the right wing of a political movement to effect dramatic constitutional changes which they could not achieve as a self-standing political party in a standard general election.[6] In the United States, at the same time, there is a new President who is by a long chalk one of the worst qualified and worst equipped individuals ever to be voted into the White House, 'defeating' – though with three million fewer votes, courtesy of the Electoral College arrangement – a candidate who by a long chalk is one of the best qualified and most relevantly experienced individuals ever to stand for the White House. By themselves these facts suggest something has gone seriously wrong in the state of democracy. They threaten to be the opening gambits in the loss of democracy altogether. Democracy must be reclaimed, in the form worked out by some of the best minds in the history of our civilization, before the opportunity to reclaim it passes.

PART I

1

THE HISTORY OF THE DILEMMA PART I

Plato, Aristotle, Machiavelli

It is customary to begin discussions of democracy with Plato's attack on it. This is appropriate, because one side of the dilemma of democracy is identified by him: the danger – in his view, the inevitability – of democracy in fact being, or at least rapidly collapsing into, rule by the least well-equipped to rule; as Plato put it on the basis of how such a process could occur in an ancient Greek city state, mob rule or rather mob anarchy – the situation for which the term *ochlocracy* was coined. That would be undesirable enough in its own right, but he took it that because democracy thus conceived is unsustainable it will, he says, with further inevitability eventuate in the restoration of order by a strongman ruler – a tyrant.

There is another danger implicit in Plato's conception of democracy, which is that of a hidden oligarchy (in our contemporary sense of rule by a group, claque or cabal) or perhaps even a hidden tyranny, capturing the reins of government under cover of democracy, by exploiting and directing sentiment through demagoguery and manipulation to achieve its own ends. This might happen even in benign ways, as was arguably the case under Pericles in the democracy of fifth century BCE Athens; but if we make the assumption, as we do in contemporary systems predicated on the idea that political authority lies with whoever counts as the enfranchised among the *demos*, hidden oligarchy would not be legitimate because it would not be democracy.

Aristotle did not see eye to eye with his teacher Plato in matters of politics. The interest in Aristotle's thought for present purposes is that he believed there to be a form of political order, which he called *polity* (in Greek *politeia*), intermediate between oligarchy and democracy, which could be described as a good or positive form of democracy if the label 'democracy' had not been placed in such bad odour by Plato that few were prepared to defend a political system under that name, not only among Plato's successors but until very recently in history. Yet the demand for wider participation in matters political that has grown in modern times in fact has considerable affinity, whether unconsciously or accidentally, with the Aristotelian notion of polity.

In the eighth book of the *Republic* Plato describes a set of political regimes arranged in descending order of merit, beginning with the kind he advocates – aristocracy, 'rule by the best' – and proceeding downhill to the worst kind, which is tyranny, rule by a single individual. 'Worst' here does not necessarily mean despotic or cruel; parts of the Greek world of Plato's time were ruled by individuals whom the nomenclature of the time designated *tyrannos*, though they might equally well have been called princes, kings, rulers, or dictators – in the neutral sense of this latter term, as used by Romans to denote the plenipotentiary leader they appointed in times of national emergency. But with the evidence before him of the actualities of tyranny, in which the licence to cruelty, murder and injustice is unrestrained either by inner virtue or outer constitutional forms, Plato viewed tyranny as the worst form of government, because, as Lord Acton long after him noted, 'Power tends to corrupt, and absolute power corrupts absolutely.' And thus the word 'tyrant' came to have a thoroughly bad connotation.

Between aristocracy and tyranny lie three intermediary forms, each a degeneration from the better form above it. *Aristocracy*, as noted, is rule by the 'best', understood not as an hereditary nobility – that was a much later misappropriation of the term – but as the most knowledgeable, virtuous and wise among the citizens, who rule disinterestedly because they have no vested interests in anything but the welfare of the state. A related form of government is *epistocracy*, rule by those who know, in other words by experts, people who are knowledgeable, experienced and educated. But the term *aristoi* means people who are not only knowledgeable and smart but highly moral. Aristocrats were Plato's 'philosopher kings', whose knowledge and virtue – which, as a subtlety of his ethical theory, are the same thing in effect – arise from grasping the nature of the eternal Good. In contemporary terms one might describe Plato's aristocrat as a kind of meritocrat, a highly intelligent and educated man, raised and trained to rule, whose dedication to his task excludes any interest in the trappings of wealth and power and even of a personal life. Indeed Plato required that the philosopher kings should have neither property nor family, but should live as, in later times, monks chose to do.

The austerity and high-mindedness of this conception explains why Plato thought there was a risk of aristocracy degenerating into *timocracy*. In modern parlance timocracy is rule by those whose qualification for government is the possession of a certain minimum of property, but in Plato's usage it denotes rule by those who seek honour, status and military glory. Unlike aristocrats, whom they somewhat resemble in being intelligent and educated, they nevertheless have an incomplete grasp of the Good, and mistake it for its outer shows – the wealth and reputation that people seek in the erroneous idea that these things are the greatest goods worth having. Whereas aristocracy would ensure stable and enduring government because no inner divisions threaten it, from timocracy downwards rivalry enters the picture, and with rivalry a greater chance of instability.

It is an easy slide from timocracy to *oligarchy*. Today this term means rule by the few – by a group, class, cabal or junta; Plato meant rule by the rich over the more numerous poor. Today an alternative label is used for this latter type of regime, viz. *plutocracy*. Timocracy degenerates into oligarchy because timocrats are permitted to accumulate private wealth, from which follow the vices that wealth encourages: pursuit of pleasure and luxury, making the possession of money seem desirable as an end in itself, and its accumulation as more important than virtue or honour. Timocrats still cared about honour, said Plato, but oligarchs only care about money.

The oligarchies of Plato's own day gave him examples of what there is to deprecate in them. If wealth is the qualification for rule, wise but poor men will be excluded from government. Class distinctions arise from the differentials in wealth, destabilizing society. Military weakness will follow, because the effete rich, denying arms to the poor for fear of insurrection, are not guaranteed to be good soldiers.

The rich enjoy a large measure of freedom because their wealth buys it for them. They have choices and personal autonomy. Envy of such freedom causes oligarchy to be overcome by *democracy*. The populace rises against the oligarchs in order to dispossess them, generally with violence and turmoil; or at best the oligarchs capitulate without a revolution, for fear of one. One way or another democracy supervenes because the many want what the few enjoyed without rival for so long. In democracy everyone claims and possesses freedom and the right to make and break laws, and that, said Plato, very soon means anarchy, for such freedom is not freedom but merely licence.

Implicit in the idea of degeneration from the best form of government, the aristocratic, is Plato's claim that the members of the *demos* lack the knowledge and virtue of the *aristoi*, which is what make the latter fit to govern. He thinks that the collapse of the democratic state is inevitable given the supposed opposite characteristics of the *polloi* or general public: ignorance, self-interest, prejudice, envy, and rivalry.

'In such a state of society', Plato writes,

> the master fears and flatters his scholars, and the scholars despise their masters and tutors; young and old are all alike; and the young man is on a level with the old, and is ready to compete with him in word or deed . . . And above all, and as the result of all, see how sensitive the citizens become; they chafe impatiently at the least touch of authority and at length, as you know, they cease to care even for the laws, written or unwritten; they will have no one over them.[1]

Accordingly democracy is no different from anarchy, or at the very least rapidly collapses into it, a situation which soon invites the intervention of a strongman to restore order. Once a strongman is in power, getting rid of him can prove difficult, and the people will be in the worst situation of all: they will live under tyranny. Thus, said Plato, do tyranny and slavery arise out of extreme forms of liberty.

*   *   *

Aristotle thought that Plato's version of aristocracy was impractical because it ignored human nature. Can there really be philosopher kings remote from the normal human desire for affection and the amenities that make life pleasant? His own idea of what would be the best kind of political order is one in which every citizen – where 'citizen' is a restricted notion meaning someone qualified to engage in the state's political life – is virtuous, equipped to attain excellence of character, and therefore able to live a life of *eudaimonia* or happiness. Such a society is in practice unlikely to exist, however, so a more modest ambition is the aforementioned *polity*. This is a mixed constitution in which no single order of citizens, whether rich, aristocratic or poor, can override the interests of the others.

In the *Nichomachean Ethics* Aristotle had defined virtue as the middle path between opposing vices – courage as the mean between cowardice and rashness, generosity as the mean between miserliness and profligacy, and so on – and he applied this philosophy of the middle ground to his idea of the best *practicable* state. Such a state will be one in which there is a large middle class, itself neither rich nor poor but occupying the territory in between, whose members will be more inclined to be fair and just than either of the other two classes because, he says, those who are moderately well off find it 'easiest to obey the rule of reason' and will be least inclined to faction.

'Large' in 'large middle class' here is a relative term. Like the Athenian democrats before him, Aristotle believed that polity is possible only in a city state small enough for the voice of the public crier, the *stentor*, to be heard all over town. In such a setting all citizens could know everything that was going on, and could know personally the men who took office as magistrates, generals or jurymen; such a society is a 'face-to-face' society.

More recent theorists have found interesting Aristotle's view that although democracy is not as good as polity because it gives an unbalancing amount of influence to the poor, who would be likely to constitute the majority, it is nevertheless the least bad of bad systems, and could be defended on the grounds that the pooled wisdom of the many might sometimes be better than the individual wisdom of the few.

Aristotle's view of democracy is not, however, as friendly to direct democracy as its invokers would like, because – like Plato before him – he anticipated most later thinking about the question of who can be a participant in political life, and gave the answer almost everyone gives, which is: 'not everyone'. The restriction is introduced through the idea of citizenship. Aristotle defined a citizen as a man who has the right to take part in the assembly, to hold office as a magistrate, and to sit on juries. Even poor men can be citizens of a state, but women, slaves and foreigners are again excluded. This in effect is the same problem, in early form, of who 'the people' are in the standard rhetoric about democracy in modern thought. I examine this crucial term in more detail later.

For Aristotle a key point was that any constitution has to be one that embodies the rule of law. The kind of democracy he most disapproved of 'is where the mass is sovereign and not the law. This kind arises when dictats are sovereign instead of the law, which happens because of demagogues. In law-abiding democracies demagogues do not arise; on the contrary, the best citizens guide. This is because the demos becomes a monarch, one person composed of many; for the many are sovereign not as individuals but collectively.'[2]

Aristotle's views on politics have not been as influential as those of Plato largely because his empirical study of constitutions, and the political theory he based on it, related to the Greek city states that were then on their way out of history. It is hard not to find compelling, though, his idea that as more citizens become educated and better off, so a democracy evolves into a polity, defined as that political order in which the pooled wisdom of reasonable and informed citizens might result in a dispensation only one notch below the ideal state *all* of whose citizens are *aristoi*, the best. The practical difficulty of achieving even this lesser ideal is one that remains a challenge for democracy today.

Herodotus makes clear that the Greeks' resistance to the Persian invasion of the early fifth century BCE was premised on the idea of freedom – *eleutheria* – which they regarded as applying peculiarly to themselves. Persians might be richer and grander, but they were slaves to their imperial overlord. In fifth century BCE Athens the goddess who personified democracy, Demokratia, was honoured alongside the city's tutelary deity, Athena. In his famous Funeral Oration delivered early in the succeeding Peloponnesian War Pericles is reported by Thucydides as saying:

> Our form of government does not enter into rivalry with the institutions of others. Our government does not copy our neighbours', but is an example to them. It is true that we are called a democracy, for the administration is in the hands of the many and not of the few. But while there exists equal justice to all and alike in their private disputes, the claim of excellence is also recognized; and when a citizen is in any way distinguished, he is preferred to the public service, not as a matter of privilege, but as the reward of merit. Neither is poverty an obstacle, but a man may benefit his country whatever the obscurity of his condition. There is no exclusiveness in our public life, and in our private business we are not suspicious of one another, nor angry with our neighbour if he does what he likes . . . While we are

thus unconstrained in our private business, a spirit of reverence pervades our public acts; we are prevented from doing wrong by respect for the authorities and for the laws, having a particular regard to those which are ordained for the protection of the injured as well as those unwritten laws which bring upon the transgressor of them the reprobation of the general sentiment.[3]

These are stirring words, so long as we forget that the 'citizens' referred to constituted less than 20% of the total population. But they can be taken to embody an aspiration which is implicitly realizable in Aristotle's idea of polity enlarging itself as more and more of the population become citizens. It is possible to read Pericles as describing an ideal for an inclusive democratic order in the contemporary world, but the actualization of a Periclean democracy today would require at least what Plato thought the *polloi* (the ordinary people) lacked – namely education, information, and a high moral sense – and what Aristotle said the middle class of a polity should exemplify: namely wisdom, pragmatism, and civic-mindedness. The practical difficulty of achieving this at the scale at which contemporary political orders exist, in large countries with populations in the tens of millions, is an intensification of the dilemma of democracy itself.

And history demonstrates that the dangers identified by Plato are genuine ones. It is a speaking fact that the dangers exist even in what are arguably the best conditions for democracy – the small city state where citizens know one another and can gather together and debate. In more populous and diverse states the same risks are much magnified. The test case for the purest form of direct democracy, namely what happens in the power vacuum following a revolution – think of the French Revolution of 1789 or the Russian Revolution of 1917 – almost always bears him out.

It is borne out even when ruling elites can no longer obstruct the masses' chance of a share in political processes by denying them education, information, mobility, and the ability to assemble with others, as was the case for example in feudal times when most people lived in conditions of serfdom. The revolutionary movements of 1789, 1848, 1917, 1949, 1956, 1968 and thereafter, in various parts of the world, were led by literate vanguards, yet few of these revolutions escaped collapse into mob rule, followed by hijacking or reprisal by tyranny.

But Plato's point does not have to be so dramatically realized in order to need addressing. It can be shown that there is a good answer to the question of how to apply the consent of the people (whoever counts as 'the people') to government of a state, by means or in structures that ensure government will be sound and stable. This answer is given in the debate about democracy from Locke to Mill, as discussed in later chapters. If Plato has done a service, it is to make the recent history of thought about politics and government at last seek to work out that answer. Looking back through the lens of hindsight, we see Aristotle as indicating the beginnings of that answer: that the participation of many, or even 'the many', is not by itself yet sufficient. It took more than two millennia to identify what the extra might be that would enable the consent of the many to be stably given, if the specified means were properly applied.

Outbursts of democratic feeling, or indeed ochlocracy with the kind of results Plato said were closely associated, are a commonplace of history. Look at a list of the uprisings and revolutions known to history, and though those identified for the period from Egypt's Second Dynasty in the third millennium BCE to around the fifth century BCE seem relatively few, no doubt because of our lack of records, from the latter date onwards scarcely a decade, and in modern times (from the sixteenth century CE) scarcely a half-decade, passes without an uprising or revolution somewhere in the world.[4] The causes might be highly various and specific, and some might be coups by elites within elites, but at least many are likely to have been expressions of the frustration of voicelessness in matters of significance, perhaps even of life and death, to those who rose up against oppression or exclusion, variously seeking to force change or at the very least demanding to be heard. The means by which ruling elites countered these movements have been less various: suppression by force, or less frequently by just enough in the way of concessions to deflate the uprising.

Of course, some rulers were overthrown and regimes or dynasties changed as a result. The succession of dynasties in China offers an example of regime change occasioned by withdrawal of consent to be governed even by voiceless and voteless masses. The so-called *Chaodai Xunhuan* (dynastic cycles) theory of Chinese history turns on an idea devised by Mencius during the Warring States period in the fifth century BCE, that of the 'Mandate of Heaven' (*Tian Ming*),[5] as what legitimizes imperial rule. Earthquakes, plagues, floods, the emperor suffering defeat in battle, suggested to his subjects that the emperor had lost *Tian Ming*. Bluntly put, it just meant that his luck had run out, and that it was therefore appropriate he should go. By one of those self-validating justifications, if a rebellion was successful it was proof that the Mandate of Heaven was on the rebels' side.

It was not always the case that popular uprisings displaced a dynasty. The Yuan Dynasty established by the Mongol leader Kublai Khan was a conquest. It was in its own turn overthrown by rebels of the Red Turban movement in the mid-fourteenth century CE. The overthrow of the Ming in 1644 was effected by a Manchu invasion, but the Ming had been weakened by an earlier peasant uprising led by Li Zicheng, who led the short-lived Shun Dynasty which the Manchus quickly swept aside in capturing the empire and establishing Qing rule. Neither the last Ming emperor, who hanged himself from a tree in the Forbidden City, nor Li himself evidently had *Tian Ming*. The Lulin rebellion against the Xin Dynasty in 17 CE was a classic peasant revolt, which followed and was followed by many such, successful and otherwise; when successful, invasions and uprisings were always regarded as having heaven's approval.[6]

At times therefore the choice of heaven was cited variously as a justification or an inducement for popular movements to turn against an imperial dynasty, as well as a *post facto* explanation for its fall. The point of mentioning this is that it is an example of the way expressions of popular consent or its absence frequently manifest themselves when other means are lacking, and of course not only in China. In practice Chinese imperial administration was not without resource in understanding how the populace was faring and how it felt; rather the contrary. But even in the best-regulated empires government is never infallible or unfellable. China's history, as affording just one example of history's frequent upsurges of popular sentiment, shows that the roots of what eventually gives rise to forms of democracy in some places are long and deep everywhere.

Rome struck a balance in the relationship between patricians and plebeians – the Senate and the people: *Senatus populusque Romanus* – which Cicero described as 'power in the people, authority in the Senate'. In the republican period of Rome's history the senators were sensible enough to know that the consent of the people was essential to their own position, and securing it was achieved both by constitutional means and by bread and circuses. The constitutional means was the tribunate, and it was a key feature in the republic's long endurance. Although the effective chief officers of state were the consuls, two men chosen each year as joint prime ministers or presidents, the populace had their own representatives with considerable powers. These were the tribunes (more accurately, the *tribuni plebis*; there were other tribunes with other functions) who were magistrates elected by the people. They were able to propose laws and had the power of veto over Senate-initiated legislation, and in general their duty was to represent the interests of the ordinary citizens. Polybius wrote: 'The tribunes are bound to do what the people resolve and chiefly to focus on their wishes.'[7] There were as many as ten in the third century BCE, though the number varied. When Augustus became emperor he absorbed the powers of the tribunate in his own person, and thereafter Roman emperors were omnipotent – unless or until assassinated.

Popular feeling did occasionally express itself more forcibly than through the filter of the tribunate. When the tribunes became too closely identified with the Senate, for example by being appointed senators after holding tribunal office, and having their powers limited during the dictatorship of Sulla, the people came out on the streets to object. The most effective form of popular activism was the *secessio plebis*, in which the ordinary citizens protested by quitting the city *en masse* – a comprehensive general strike – thereby closing all shops and facilities, and leaving the patricians to fend for themselves. Between the beginning of the fifth century BCE and 287 BCE there were about half a dozen secessions. The last of them was the celebrated occasion on which the citizens forced the Senate to accept the *lex Hortensia* giving plebiscites legal force.

One could not describe Rome's political arrangements as a democracy in the republican period, but it was a compromise which gave the people a voice that could be heard with effect. Even more important, perhaps, was the fact that Roman law secured the liberties of citizens in significantly worthwhile ways. It is no wonder that acquiring Roman citizenship was considered a great and desirable prize for those not born Roman. The privileges and protections of citizenship survived the transition from republic to empire, and lasted for several centuries more; that is a testament to the robustness and common sense of Roman institutions. In large part this was owing to the inclusiveness and tolerance of Rome; differences of ethnicity, language and religion were of no importance from the law's point of view. The laws of the city operated alongside the 'law of peoples' (*ius gentium*), that is, the laws and customs of the other peoples of the empire.

Long after Rome had become an empire not just in extent but in being ruled by an emperor, legal authorities still paid lip service to the idea of popular consent to imperial rule. Writing in the third century CE the Roman jurist Ulpianus, when stating the principle that became a cornerstone of law for centuries afterwards because it was incorporated in the *Codex Justinianus* (the Justinian Code, promulgated in the sixth century CE), namely *quod principi placuit legis habet vigorem*, 'what pleases the prince has the force of law', felt obliged to add 'because the Roman people have conferred on him their authority and power'.[8]

It was not, however, the masses that brought the firstlings of democratic thought to life in Europe and through Europe eventually to other parts of the world. The parliaments that existed in medieval England and France were assemblies of nobles and divines, not bodies representing the interest of plebeians. Kings were *primus inter pares*, first among equals; Crown and nobility were like Mafia families that held power because they were powerful (might is right), owned the land, and divided and held in subjugation the rest of the populace. Political activity was confined to the internecine quarrels of one group of barons against another, usually over which of them could get hold of the crown for one of their own members, as for example in England's Wars of the Roses in the fifteenth century.

With larger wars, larger armies, and greater need for taxation to pay for both, power became more centralized and kings therefore more powerful, to the detriment of the barons. When that happened a new justification for kingly power was needed in place of election by the baronage. It was provided by the doctrine of 'the divine right of kings'. This was a doctrine that John Locke felt he had to refute in the 1680s by unpicking the arguments of Sir Robert Filmer, in order to provide a defence of the power of parliament to replace the power of a deity in saying who shall be king. Locke's views, in turn, were made possible by the emergence of ideas predicated on Renaissance recovery and adaptation of lessons learned from classical antiquity. The thinker chiefly responsible for this was Niccolo Machiavelli.

Machiavelli's reputation might rest mainly on his notorious prompt-book for the 'Machiavellian' ruler, *The Prince* (1513, first printed in 1532), but for present purposes the more relevant text is his *Discourses* (1517, first printed in 1531). In the former he had argued that a ruler must be uncompromising to the point of crime in creating a state and defending it in times of emergency, but in the *Discourses* he turns attention to ensuring the durability and stability of a state, which, he argues, is achieved by involving the citizens in the welfare of the city and trusting them to bear arms in defence of it, thus encouraging patriotism. The unreliable practice of hiring mercenary armies had in part been prompted by fear of arming one's own citizenry lest they rise in revolt, but the lesson of antiquity, said Machiavelli, is that strong republics are those which harness the power of their citizens. 'Every city should provide ways for the people to follow their ambitions', he wrote, 'especially if the city wishes to benefit from their commitment in great undertakings.'[9]

Machiavelli's appeal to antiquity is explicit. The full title of the work is *Discourses upon the First Ten Books of Livy*, and he begins it by saying: 'Those who read what the beginning of the City of Rome was, and of her Lawgivers and how it was organized, do not wonder that so much virtu had been maintained for so many centuries by the city.' *Virtu* is Machiavelli's term for the talent, energy, commitment, and sense of purpose that distinguish a great leader and a vigorous populace. The first lesson he drew from Livy's history is what he saw as the healthy 'disunion' of Rome's plebeians and Senate. Between the expulsion of the Tarquins and the election of tribunes there had been tumults and dissensions between plebeians and patricians, among other things prompting secessions of the former as described above; but, Machiavelli says, 'if the tumults were the cause of creation of Tribunes, they merit the highest praise, for in addition to giving the people a part in administration, they were established for guarding Roman liberty.' Accordingly he argues that lively political participation is a strengthener, not a threat, to a state seeking to grow large and powerful: Rome

> gave the Plebs strength and increased power and infinite opportunities for tumults. And if the Roman State had been more tranquil, it would have resulted that she would have become feeble, because there would have been cut off from her the means of being able to attain that greatness which she achieved.

So that Rome wanting to remove the causes for tumults, would also take away the causes for expansion.

Commentators often point out that Machiavelli's theories were predicated on his familiarity with the Renaissance city state, similar in many respects to the *poleis* of Greek antiquity. And indeed he cites the examples of Sparta, and for a contemporary instance Venice, as small states which, as a result of their organization, were stable while they were content to be small. But:

> If anyone sought to establish a new Republic, he should have to consider if he wished to expand in dominion and power as did Rome, or whether it should remain within narrow limits. In the first case, it is necessary to establish it as Rome, and to give place to tumults and general dissensions as best he can; for without a great number of men, and those well armed, no Republic can ever increase, or if it did increase, to maintain itself. In the second case he may establish her as Sparta and Venice: but because expansion is the poison of such Republics, he ought in every way he can prevent her from making acquisitions, for such acquisitions, based on a weak Republic, are entirely their ruin.

For present purposes the implication is that involvement of the populace in the ambitions of the state requires accepting and managing the 'tumults' that will arise. Only in a small state can the people be suppressed. For Machiavelli these considerations related to state ambition, but they were inadvertently prescient from a different point of view: as populations grew, and in the succeeding centuries as literacy, awareness and, later, nationalism grew with them, so the need to involve more of the people in ways that gave a voice to their interests and ambitions grew too. The Roman model, in Machiavelli's terms, increasingly turned out to be the one from which the relevant lessons were best learned.

Machiavelli's way of putting the point about lively debate, disagreement, and clashes of views and policies, together resulting in the health of the state, is a partial description of what a democratic order needs. Democracy is not just elections, and can sometimes even exist *de facto* without them; but essential to anything worthy of the name is the possibility of debate, freedom of expression and assembly, and a due process of law which protects people from arbitrary arrest and punishment, most especially in connection with matters of opinion.[10] Although Machiavelli saw the participation of the populace as being necessary if a republic is to endure and increase, he did not go so far as to suggest anything resembling enfranchisement of the populace, or part of it, as a way of doing something further and different: conferring power on government by their ballot. It was another century and a half before a demand for a right to do so was explicitly made.

2

THE HISTORY OF THE DILEMMA PART II

The Putney Debates, 1647

Democracy as a practical idea, though the word was not used, came vividly into view during the English Civil War. In the late summer of 1647, at the end of the first phase of the Civil War when Charles I had been captured and imprisoned in his palace at Hampton Court, officers and men of the New Model Army met in a church at Putney outside London to debate the basis for a peace settlement with the king. It was an extraordinary event, in the literal sense of 'extraordinary'; there had quite probably been nothing like it since debates in the Athenian *agora* two millennia before. Neither Wat Tyler nor Jack Cade in the rebellions of 1381 and 1450 respectively had sought universal adult male suffrage and annual parliaments. For the activists in the Peasants' Revolt of the earlier date it was enough for the rebels – apart from their desire to kill some of the most hated of the king's ministers; which they did – to seek freedom both from the poll tax and serfdom, and to be granted amnesty for their revolt.

If there were aspects of the Peasants' Revolt that foreshadowed political demands as such, it was for freedom and equality for all men, and a restoration of the 'Law of Winchester'. This latter was a provision that had in effect permitted local communities to govern themselves according to their own local traditions. It has been interpreted more narrowly as a demand that locally traditional punishments be applied to criminals – in Winchester itself castration and blinding had been substituted for hanging as the punishment for serious crimes – but the intent must have been wider. The desire for abolition of serfdom or villeinage, practices by which peasants were tied to the land of the lord they served, were expressed as a desire for general equality; in a sermon preached to the rebels on Blackheath Common the rebels' priest John Ball asked: 'When Adam dug and Eve span, who was then the gentleman?'

This same question was on the lips of the Levellers at Putney three centuries later. The name 'Leveller' had originally applied to rural dwellers ousted from the land by the enclosures of the sixteenth and early seventeenth centuries, who in protest cut down or 'levelled' hedges planted to enclose property. In the Civil War the term came to denote those, both members of the New Model Army and civilians, who took the opportunity of the time to argue for extensive reforms. They wanted (almost) universal male suffrage, biennial elections, fairer taxation, equal treatment before the law, legal proceedings to be in English, abolition of monopolies, abolition of tithes, religious tolerance, and a written constitution. The demands were set out in documents collectively called 'An Agreement of the People', an early draft of which was read – indeed probably written – and discussed at Putney.

The New Model Army had come into being in 1645 as a combination of three Parliamentary forces under the command of Sir Thomas Fairfax, with Oliver Cromwell as his Lieutenant-General of cavalry. Its soldiery were much prone either to prayer or desertion, but even so proved more effective in this form than before the reorganization. It won the battle of Naseby in June 1645, and after several follow-up victories obliged Charles I to surrender at Oxford in the following June.

The king's surrender was expected to result in a negotiation between him and Parliament, with peace to follow. But Charles was in no mood to negotiate, merely pretending to do so while his forces were reorganizing themselves. At the same time the Presbyterian faction in Parliament angered the New Model Army by refusing to meet demands for back pay and settlement of other grievances, by plans for sending it to Ireland, and by plans for an uncongenial Scottish-style religious settlement in England. Mutinous mutterings began to spread through the New Model Army, so because it represented only half the total Parliamentary forces, the Presbyterians in Parliament decided to disband it. This increased the troops' sense of grievance, and a process began by which each regiment elected two or more 'agitators' or agents who met to organize the Army's campaign of complaint. Parliament passed a 'Declaration of Dislike' describing complainers and petitioners as 'enemies of the state', and began to think of bringing other Parliamentary forces to readiness in case the New Model Army had to be repressed by force. New Model determination was yet further stiffened by these moves.

To keep the Army together and disciplined, its most senior officers – the 'Grandees' – combined with representatives of the 'agitators' into a General Council of the Army. The Army marched towards London, but in order not to provoke Parliament too far it camped outside, near Putney, a village on the Thames to the west of the city. Here between 28 October and 11 November 1647 the Putney Debates, as they became known, took place.

The Army Grandees had issued their own document, entitled the 'Heads of the Proposals', as a basis for a peace negotiation with Charles I. More moderate in content than the demands being made of Charles by the Presbyterians in Parliament, it nevertheless asked for changed constituency boundaries and two-year parliaments. Charles preferred it to the Presbyterians' demands. But the 'Proposals' did not satisfy the Levellers, whose aims were much more ambitious.

To begin with, the point of the meetings in Putney was for the Grandees to consider a document called 'The Case of the Army Truly Stated', which had been presented to them as an account of the soldiers' grievances and desires. The Grandees were not minded to accept the demands set out in 'The Case', and indeed some of them recommended arresting and hanging the authors. But wiser thoughts prevailed, and a committee was appointed to examine the document so that a considered reply could be offered. The Grandees then asked the agents of the Army to discuss their reply. On 27 October one of the Army agents, Robert Everard, brought not only a reply to the Grandees' reply, but a copy of a document entitled 'An Agreement of the People for a Firme and Present Peace, upon the Grounds of Common-right and Freedome', probably written that very day to grasp the opportunity for advancing the Levellers' cause.

The 'Agreement' begins:

Having by our late labours and hazards made it appear to the world at how high a rate we value our just freedom, and God having so far owned our cause as to deliver the enemies thereof into our hands, we do now hold ourselves as bound in mutual duty to each other to take the best care we can for the future to avoid both the danger of returning into a slavish condition and the chargeable remedy of another war; for, as it cannot be imagined that so many of our countrymen would have opposed us in this quarrel if they had understood their own good, so may we safely promise to ourselves that when our common rights and liberties shall be cleared, their endeavours will be disappointed that seek to make themselves our masters.[1]

The boldness of the demands that followed is explained by the fact that the Levellers now found themselves in a high stakes situation. They had sent a petition to Parliament earlier in the year which the Presbyterian majority had caused to be burned by the public hangman in token of their emphatic rejection of it. This made it clear to the Levellers that their best chance was the Army. The difficulty they faced was the reluctance of the Army's Grandees – Fairfax, Cromwell, and Henry Ireton chief among them – to agree to their demands, and also the fact that the soldiers' pay (which was in arrears) could only come through the Army bureaucracy, controlled by headquarters. The Army was anyway not a united body; only some of the regiments were fully behind the Levellers, many of the common soldiers were not interested in larger political questions anyway, and a further many were religious radicals whose devotion to prayer and millennial beliefs meant that their gaze was fixed on far less worldly matters.

Fairfax was ill and unable to attend the Putney meetings, so they were chaired by Cromwell with his son-in-law Ireton at his side. Cromwell said, on reading the 'Agreement', that he saw 'there were new designs a-driving', and asked that the authors come to discuss them with the General Council. Because the Leveller movement was at that point new and unfamiliar – later he was to be unhesitating in repressing them – and because piety lay heavy on his conscience (might the voice of God be speaking through the document?) Cromwell thought it best to try an irenic approach. From the Levellers' point of view, presenting the 'Agreement' so precipitously turned out to be a tactical error, because in going beyond the Army's 'Case', itself more radical than the Grandees' own 'Heads', it was immediately seen as divisive and unhelpful.

The point for present purposes is the conception of democracy that the 'Agreement' embodied. Far ahead of its time, many of its principles and even some of its actual demands have indeed become realities in the centuries since. But in its own day it amazed by the sheer extent of its boldness. After reading it Cromwell said: 'Truly this paper does contain in it very great alterations of the very government of the Kingdom, alterations from that government that it hath been under, I believe I may almost say since it was a nation.' His appeal to the past was of course irrelevant; his next point was more germane: 'Although the pretensions in it and the expression in it are very plausible, how do we know if whilst we are disputing these things another company of men shall gather together, and they shall put out a paper as plausible perhaps as this? And not only another, and another, but many of this kind?' This point touches a nerve: how do you create a democracy if not democratically; by what authority do the authors of the 'Agreement' claim that it is an agreement 'of the people'?

After its sonorous opening the 'Agreement' proceeded to set out demands for a better proportionality of electoral constituencies, biennial parliaments chosen by 'the people', religious toleration, freedom from military conscription, equality before the law, and an amnesty for all engaged in 'the late public differences'. All these things 'we declare to be our native rights; and therefore are agreed and resolved to maintain them with our utmost possibilities'.

There followed a letter to the people of England, asking them to join with the drafters in declaring that the demands are for 'our native rights', and explaining that

> if any shall inquire why we should desire to join in an agreement with the people to declare these to be our native rights — and not rather petition to the parliament for them — the reason is evident. No Act of parliament is or can be unalterable, and so cannot be sufficient security to save you or us harmless from what another parliament may determine if it should be corrupted. And besides, parliaments are to receive the extent of their power and trust from those that betrust them; and therefore the people are to declare what their power and trust is – which is the intent of this agreement. And it's to be observed that though there has formerly been many Acts of parliament for the calling of parliaments every year, yet you have been deprived of them and enslaved through want of them. And therefore, both necessity for your security in these freedoms that are essential to your well-being, and woeful experience of the manifold miseries and distractions that have been lengthened out since the war ended through want of such a settlement, require this agreement. And *when* you and we shall be joined together therein we shall readily join with you to petition the parliament – as they are our fellow-commoners equally concerned – to join with us.

The 'Agreement' was signed 'Your most faithful fellow-commoners now in arms for your service', followed by the names of ten serving soldiers of the New Model Army.

The second day of the debates at Putney, 29 October 1647, is the famous day. Discussion began over the first clause, demanding that representation in Parliament should be proportional to the number of inhabitants in a constituency rather than being, as the Grandees' 'Heads' demanded, proportional to taxation – which of course implied a property or wealth qualification for the right to vote. Cromwell and Ireton defended the latter position, Ireton saying that only those with a 'permanent fixed interest in this Kingdom', landowners and members of Corporations, were entitled to the franchise. In fact this implied a restriction of the then existing franchise; in the counties there was a 40 shilling freehold qualification for the vote, which in some places was not often checked, with the result that all the male householders voted in elections.

The spokesmen on the 'Agreement' side were Thomas Rainborough, a colonel of an infantry regiment in the New Model Army, and John Wildman, a civilian Leveller who was probably the author of the 'Agreement'. Rainborough replied to Ireton's assertion that the vote should belong to those with property by arguing that nobody should be obliged to obey a government he had not had a voice in choosing, and he asked what the soldiers had been fighting for if it was just to put themselves back under the control of the rich. The soldiers, Ireton responded, have been fighting to curb the power of a despot.

The exchange between Ireton and Rainborough not only contains a celebrated remark by the latter which goes to the very heart of the point of democracy, but it encapsulates the resistance that the concept of a universal franchise for so long met.

Ireton began by remarking on the demand in the opening section of the 'Agreement' for representation to be proportional to the (male) inhabitants of a constituency: 'This doth make me think that the meaning is that every man that is an inhabitant is to be equally considered, and to have an equal voice in the election of representers, the persons that are for the general

Representative; and if that be the meaning then I have something to say against it.' Rainborough replied:

Really I think that the poorest he that is in England hath a life to live as the greatest he; and therefore truly, Sir, I think it's clear that every man that is to live under a Government ought first by his own consent to put himself under that Government; and I do think that the poorest man in England is not at all bound in a strict sense to that Government that he hath not had a voice to put himself under; and I am confident that when I have heard the reasons against it, something will be said to answer those reasons, in so much that I should doubt whether he was an Englishman or no that should doubt of these things.

Ireton replied:

If you make this the rule I think you must fly for refuge to an absolute natural right, and you must deny all civil right ... For my part I think it is no right at all. I think no person hath a right to an interest or share in the disposing of the affairs of the Kingdom, and in determining or choosing those that shall determine what laws we shall be ruled by here. No person hath a right to this, that hath not a permanent fixed interest in this Kingdom; and those persons together are properly the represented of this Kingdom, and consequently are to make up the representers of this Kingdom, who taken together do comprehend whatsoever is of real or permanent interest in the Kingdom. And I am sure I cannot tell what any man can say why a foreigner coming in amongst us ... should not as well lay claim to it as any other.

Ireton saw that the Leveller argument was premised on the idea of birthright, and continued:

Men may justly have by birthright, by their very being born in England, that we should not seclude them out of England, that we should not refuse to give them air and place and ground, and the freedom of the highways and other things to live amongst us, not any man that is born here, though by his birth there come nothing to him that is part of permanent interest of this Kingdom . . . But that by a man's being born here he shall have a share in that power that shall dispose of the lands here, and of all things here, I do not think it a sufficient ground . . . Those that choose the representors for the making of laws by which this State and Kingdom are to be governed are the persons who taken together do comprehend the local interest of this Kingdom; that is, the persons in whom all land lies, and those in Corporations in whom all trading lies . . . If we shall go to take away this [fundamental part of the civil constitution] we shall plainly go to take away all property and interest that any man hath.

Rainborough replied:

I say that either it must be the law of God or the law of man that must prohibit the meanest man in the Kingdom to have this benefit as well as the greatest. I do not find anything in the law of God that a Lord shall choose twenty burgesses and a gentleman but two, or a poor man shall choose none. I find no such thing in the law of nature, nor in the law of nations. But I do find that all Englishmen must be subject to English laws, and I do verily believe that there is no man but will say that the foundation of all law lies in the people, and if [it lie] in the people, I am to seek for this exemption [that is, what exempts people from the right to vote].

He then pointed out that many of the men who had fought against the king in the war had so left their property to decay that they were no longer worth the 40 shillings that gave them a vote; how could fighting for the cause deprive them of what the cause itself was about?

Ireton argued that if all people had a right to vote by 'the right of nature' then 'you must deny all property too', for if all have the right to vote then 'by the same right of nature, he hath the same [equal] right in any goods he sees: meat, drink, clothes, to take and use them for his sustenance . . . He hath the [same] freedom to anything that anyone doth account himself to have any property in. Possibly I may not have so real a regard to the peace of the Kingdom as that man who hath a permanent interest in it. He that is here today and gone tomorrow, I do not see that he hath such a permanent interest.'

Rainborough responded:

If I have no interest in the Kingdom I must suffer by all their laws be they right or wrong. Nay thus: a gentleman lives in a country and hath three or four lordships – God knows how they got them – and when a Parliament is called he must be a Parliament man; and it may be he sees some poor men, they live near this man, he can crush them . . . God hath set down that thing as to property with this law of his, 'Thou shalt not steal.' . . . I wish you would not make the world believe that we are for anarchy.

The debate went back and forth in these terms until a man called Rich interjected that Ireton had a point:

You have five to one in this Kingdom that have no permanent interest. Some men have ten, some twenty servants. If the master and servant shall be equal electors, then clearly those that have no interest in the Kingdom will make it their interest to choose that have no interest. It may happen that the majority may by law, not in a confusion, destroy property; there may be a law enacted that there shall be an equality of goods and estate.

This last idea made Ireton expostulate: 'Though I shall acquiesce in having no property, yet I cannot give my heart or hand to it; because it is a thing evil in itself and scandalous to the world, and I desire this Army may be free from both.' And that in turn drew a sharp response from Edward Sexby, one of the principal 'agitators' of the Army who pulled no punches in the debate:

We have engaged in this Kingdom and ventured our lives, and it was all for this: to recover our birthrights and privileges as Englishmen and by the arguments urged there is none. There are many thousands of us soldiers that have ventured our lives; we have had little property in the Kingdom as to our estates, yet we have had a birthright. But it seems now except a man hath a fixed estate in this Kingdom, he hath no right in this Kingdom. I wonder we were so much deceived. If we had not a right to the Kingdom, we were mere mercenary soldiers . . . I am resolved to give my birthright to none . . . I do think the poor and meaner of this Kingdom have been the means of the preservation of this Kingdom.

Ireton: 'If a man mean by birthright, whatsoever he can challenge by the law of nature, suppose there were no constitution at all, supposing no civil law and civil constitution . . . you leave no property, nor no foundation for any man to enjoy anything.'

Rainborough: 'Sir, I see that it is impossible to have liberty but that all property must be taken away. If it be laid down for a rule, and if you will say it, it must be so. But I would fain know what the soldier has fought for all this while? He hath fought to enslave himself, to give power to men of riches, men of estates, to make him a perpetual slave.'

Ireton: 'I tell you what the soldier of the Kingdom hath fought for. The danger that we stood in was, that one man's will must be a law . . . that is, that the will of one man should not be a law, but that the law of this Kingdom should be by a choice of persons to represent, and that choice to be made by the generality of the Kingdom. Here was a right that induced men to fight . . . Liberty may be had and property not be destroyed.'

At this point Cromwell intervened to complain of the intemperateness of Sexby, saying as he did so that he and Ireton of course agreed that the franchise should be extended and made more equitable, but not, as Ireton earlier insisted, 'beyond all bounds' and certainly not at risk to the rights of property. Sexby replied:

I am sorry that my zeal to what I apprehend is good should be so ill resented . . . Do you not think it were a sad and miserable condition that we have fought all this time for nothing? All here both great and small do think that we fought for something. I confess many of us fought for those ends which we since saw were not those which caused us to go through difficulties and straits to venture all in the ship with you. It had been good in you to have advertised us of it, and I believe you would have had fewer under your command to be commanded . . . I think there are many that have not estates that in honesty have as much right in the freedom of their choice as any that have great estates . . . It was the ground that we took up arms [on], and it is the ground which we shall maintain.

Talk of the original or ancient rights of Englishmen had vaguely behind it a view that before the Norman Conquest – the

Normans being the ancestors of most of the aristocracy and landed gentry – there had been a time when the English enjoyed a native liberty and self-determination that the Normans had taken away. There was something of the myth of the Golden Age behind this, perhaps reaching even further back to a prototypical conception of a State of Nature in which all men were equal and private property did not exist. 'Men' of course meant the male of the species, as it did throughout the Putney discussion; the rights of women did not surface in debate until the end of the following century.

The demands of the Levellers were not, however, for the restoration of supposed ancient rights, but related to the circumstances of their present day. A war had been fought against the absolutism of a monarch, and the opportunity it offered was a remaking of the constitution to give all men a voice, independently of considerations about property or heredity. The Levellers most certainly did not see the war as being waged in order to shift power from the Crown to the propertied class, as if it were just the next chapter after Runnymede. There the barons had wrested concessions from the Crown; here those with property and the voice it gave them were wresting further concessions for a wider class, but still not for everyone; indeed it mattered to this class, as Ireton's arguments show, that the franchise should not go to the unpropertied lest the unpropertied interfere with property by seeking either to redistribute or abolish it. The acute sense of injustice conveyed by Sexby's remarks indicate the clarity with which he and other Levellers saw what the division of opinion fundamentally turned upon. And Rainborough was accordingly prompted to say that Ireton's argument showed there could be no liberty while there was property.

Ireton's responses to Rainborough's argument that 'the poorest he' had as much right to choose the government under which he lived as 'the richest he', are as modern as the Levellers' arguments themselves, in the sense that he did not say that the poor and unpropertied were not fit to vote because they were most likely uneducated and even illiterate – an anticipatory version of political correctness prevented him from quoting Plato to that effect. Instead he insisted on the defining feature of those likely to have the relevant degree of knowledge and competence, namely that they were likely to live above the qualifying property level for enfranchisement. Rainborough and his fellows likewise did not seek to argue that 'the poorest he' was as informed, knowledgeable and competent to use a vote wisely as 'the richest he', but simply that as a man under government he had a right to a voice in that government. But the underlying argument comes down to the same point: democracy, though the word was not used, was associated with ochlocracy, and as such the demand for it put at risk the imperative need for an arrangement that would maximize chances for sound and stable government while harvesting as much consent for it as would be consistent with that end.

The Putney Debates did not get far enough to consider whether there could be mechanisms that made popular democracy consistent with sound and stable government. They left unresolved the problem of masters coercing their servants to vote as the masters wished, by not considering the remedy of secret ballots. And it occurred to none of them that the poorest she, by the same argument as defended the right of the poorest he, had as much right as he for a say.

Nevertheless, the demand for universal male suffrage was by itself revolutionary enough to ensure that there would sooner rather than later be a reaction against the Leveller cause. The Levellers issued pamphlets and published a newspaper, the *Moderate*, gaining an increased following in the two years after the Putney Debates. The writing was, however, on the wall for them as early as a mere month after Putney, when Fairfax and Cromwell decided to push forward with the 'Heads of the Proposals' rather than the 'Agreement of the People' as the Army's manifesto. At an Army meeting soldiers who protested against this decision were arrested and their leader executed. Thereafter the Army accepted the Grandees' decision. The height of the Levellers' influence was reached when a large crowd demonstrated in London on the day of Thomas Rainborough's funeral in October 1648. But after the trial and execution of Charles I in 1649 the new government, heavily under the influence of the Army and with Cromwell as chairman of the Council of State, moved to arrest the leading Levellers and to suppress those units in the Army that mutinied in support of them. This brought the Leveller movement to an end.

3

THE BEGINNINGS OF
THE SOLUTION PART I

Locke, Hobbes, Spinoza

Revolutionary circumstances had given rise to the ideas debated at Putney, and further revolutionary circumstances were the prompt for one of the most influential political tracts written in the seventeenth century, John Locke's *Two Treatises on Government*. Hobbes' great work, *Leviathan*, and Spinoza's unfinished masterpiece, the *Tractatus Theologico-Politicus*, are both classics of political studies, but they did not shape the history of actual political events as Locke's writings did, for these were quoted verbatim and at length in the revolutionary writings of eighteenth-century America and France.

It is a matter of scholarly controversy whether Locke wrote the *Treatises*, or at least the second and more important of them, before or after the Glorious Revolution of 1688. If afterwards, they were written as *post facto* justification. If before, they were written as *enabling* justification. They were not published until afterwards, but in the period of Locke's self-imposed exile in the

Netherlands, where he had sought sanctuary from the danger of arrest for his opposition to the prospect of James II succeeding to the throne, his ideas might have reached others in manuscript. In any event, both in their rejection of absolutism, and in their exposition and defence of a form of representative government, Locke's writings were especially congenial to the revolutionaries of the following century.

The crucial question for political thought is: what confers authority on government? Democracy says 'the people' (in some sense of 'the people') and how their will finds expression. In much of history authority was a matter of might; power lay with the strongest arm. But after feudalism, when the ruler had ceased to be merely an individual drawn from among a peerage of barons, so that he or she was now ruling with greater central-ized power, a new justification was needed, and it was provided by the doctrine of 'divine right'.

This view originated in the Church's view that Christendom is a single domain to which individual kingdoms are subordi-nate. The Pope's imprimatur was a useful possession, even if kings chafed under the idea that they were subordinate to the throne of St Peter, because it helped to settle disputes over successions, and justified suppression of challenges to their authority.

But when Christendom fragmented in the Reformation much strife ensued, at length settled – to some degree at least – by acceptance of the Augsburg Principle that subjects were to accept the confession of their rulers: *cuius regio, eius religio* – the religion of the ruler is the religion of the people. Here 'people' unequivocally meant 'everyone'. In Protestant states there was no Pope to channel divine sanction through the laying on of hands; that sanction had now to be viewed as coming directly from God. But the principle remained that kings were divinely appointed and that allegiance to them was therefore a religious duty.

Jacques-Bénigne Bossuet was the writer who provided justification for Louis XIV's absolutist style of monarchy, citing scriptural passages that unequivocally support a divine right theory. Proverbs 8:15–16 says 'By me kings reign, and princes decree justice. By me princes rule, and nobles, even all the judges of the earth.' In Romans 13:1–2 St Paul says 'Let every soul be subject unto the higher powers. For there is no power but of God. Whosoever therefore resisteth the power, resisteth the ordinance of God: and they that resist shall receive to themselves damnation.' Bossuet wrote:

> We have already seen that all power is of God. The ruler, adds St Paul, 'is the minister of God to thee for good. But if thou do that which is evil, be afraid; for he beareth not the sword in vain; for he is the minister of God, a revenger to execute wrath upon him that doeth evil.' Rulers then act as the ministers of God and as his lieutenants on earth. It is through them that God exercises his empire. Think you 'to withstand the kingdom of the Lord in the hand of the sons of David'? Consequently, as we have seen, the royal throne is not the throne of a man but the throne of God himself. The Lord 'hath chosen Solomon my son to sit upon the throne of the kingdom of Israel.' And again, 'Solomon sat on the throne of the Lord.' . . . It appears from all this that the person of the king is sacred, and that to attack him in any way is sacrilege. God has the kings anointed by his prophets with the holy unction in like manner as he has his bishops and altars anointed . . . Kings should be guarded as holy things, and whosoever neglects to protect them is worthy of death . . . The royal power is absolute . . . The prince need render account of his acts to no one.[1]

Bossuet was not an unintelligent apologist for this view; he did not confuse the different concepts of *absolute* power and *arbitrary* power.

> But kings, although their power comes from on high, should not regard themselves as masters of that power to use it at their pleasure . . . they must use it with fear and self-restraint, as a thing coming from God and of which God will demand an account . . . Kings should tremble then as they use the power God has granted them; and let them think how horrible is the sacrilege if they use for evil a power which comes from God. We behold kings seated upon the throne of the Lord, bearing in their hands the swords which God himself has given them. What profanation, what arrogance, for the unjust king to sit on God's throne to render decrees contrary to his laws and to use the sword which God has put in his hand for deeds of violence and to slay his children![2]

The interesting implication of this view is that a king is not absolutely absolute; the implication must be that if he misuses his power he violates God's law, and therefore forfeits the right to rule. Can he be obliged by the Church to abdicate therefore? Can the people resist him? The question was complicated by the possibility of an analogy with the Church doctrine that says that once a priest is ordained it does not matter whether he sins, for he can still administer the sacraments because the powers conferred on him by ordination exist independently of his fallen nature. Is this also the case with anointed kings? Louis XIV regarded his right to rule as inalienable, thus giving an affirmative answer to the question. But this was not what all Protestant theologians thought, an uncomfortable view for Protestant rulers therefore, if questions arose about their administration of a state's affairs.

An implication of absolutism is that because kings answer only to the deity, they are not bound by promises to mortals, including other monarchs – which in Louis XIV's opinion conveniently meant that he did not have to be bound by international treaties any longer than it was expedient to be so. It also meant that a king is above the law, indeed that the Ulpian principle of 'what pleases the prince is the law' applies.

The Glorious Revolution of 1688 in England was a complete rejection of these doctrines, and in their place was substituted the principle of parliamentary government. Parliament chose to regard James II's absconding as abdicating, and therefore announced that the throne was vacant. It invited William of Orange to occupy it along with James's daughter Mary – thus providing a fig-leaf of hereditary succession – but only after complex negotiations about William's powers once he assumed the crown. Parliament, thus, had taken the place of God as the source of political authority. Notice the import of those words: *Parliament* now stood in the place of the deity, not those few enfranchised electors who voted for some of the members of part of Parliament.

It is questionable whether this turn of events would have been possible without the power exercised by Parliament in its struggle with the Crown in the Civil War. In the first decade after Charles II's restoration in 1660 the so-called 'Cavalier Parliament' began by being quiescent and highly Royalist, with the House of Lords as the chief driver of government. But after 1670 the House of Commons increasingly asserted its independence. As anxieties about Charles II's religious sympathies grew, and sharper anxieties about a Catholic monarch ascending the throne in the shape of James II, the political atmosphere in England darkened. Locke's patron, the Earl of Shaftesbury, who had served as a minister in Charles II's government, joined the opposition and then had to flee into exile for fear of arrest, dying in the Netherlands in 1683. Locke himself fell under suspicion following the Rye House affair – a plot to assassinate Charles II and his brother James, Duke of York, together – and had to flee to the Netherlands, where he remained until returning to England in the same ship carrying William III's consort Queen Mary in 1688.

The Glorious Revolution turned on two intimately connected points: the sovereignty of Parliament and the repudiation of the doctrine of divine right. By crowning William on its own terms Parliament had put in place a new constitutional settlement. It now controlled the nation's finances and its armed forces, which meant that it controlled everything. In addition the Bill of Rights secured the independence of the judiciary and a right to petition, both of them bulwarks of a free society.

When he prepared his *Treatises* for the press Locke added a preface saying that his aim was to justify the choice of William as king. The *Treatises* will, said Locke, 'make good his title in the consent of the people', using Sir William Temple's phrase 'the consent of the people' but by 'the people' meaning, of course, Parliament and the classes and interests represented in it.

The *First Treatise* is a full-length refutation of Sir Robert Filmer's *Patriarchia*, a defence of the divine right doctrine. Absolute monarchy is derived by Filmer from the authority given by God to Adam in Eden, an arrangement intended, said Filmer, to apply to Adam and his heirs for all time. Locke patiently tracked Filmer through the minutiae of history to refute him at each turn, his reason for expending so much effort on the task being that a far more important target lay behind Filmer's argument, namely Hobbes.

The subtitle of Filmer's book is 'A defence of the Natural Power of Kings against the Unnatural Liberty of the People'. He had written it in Charles I's reign, but published it only in 1680, when it was being argued that James, Duke of York, should not be permitted to follow Charles II onto the throne because he was a Roman Catholic. Filmer followed Bossuet in citing scriptural precedents in support of divine right theory, and said that he and Hobbes were at one on 'the Right of exercising government' though he disagreed with him about how that right is acquired, Filmer saying that it is endowed by God and passed on through inheritance, whereas for Hobbes it is acquired when individuals voluntarily forfeit their liberty in return for security.

Locke did not mention Hobbes directly because he was believed to be an atheist, and atheists were viewed with such repugnance that they were not mentioned in polite conversation. More to the point, however, Hobbes' views applied equally to republican as to monarchical regimes, so he could be as well cited by anyone defending William's right to the throne of England as by those opposing his right.

Hobbes viewed membership of society as the only genuine guarantee of individual safety. Without it, living in a 'state of nature', people would prey on each other and life would be 'nasty, poor, brutish and short'. Not even mutual self-defence agreements among individuals would help: 'be there never so great a multitude; yet if their actions be directed according to their particular judgements, and particular appetites, they can expect thereby no defence, no protection, neither against a common enemy, nor against the injuries of another.'[3]

Safety lay only in the existence of a 'common power' with complete authority, said Hobbes, and he named it 'Leviathan'. Its authority is derived from the agreement of every member of society to accept its unrestricted power over them. The Leviathan could be an individual, such as a monarch, a group, or any other body, just so long as it has complete power:

> For by this authority, given him by every particular man in the commonwealth, he hath the use of so much power and strength conferred on him, that by terror thereof, he is enabled to form the wills of them all, to peace at home, and mutual aid against their enemies abroad. And in him consisteth the essence of the commonwealth which is, to define it, *one person, of whose acts a great multitude, by mutual covenant one with another, have made themselves every one the author, to the end he may use the strength and means of them all, as he shall think expedient, for their peace and common defence.*[4]

Leviathan owes no obligations to the people once constituted, beyond acting for their safety. So that it can fulfil this function properly, Hobbes says it must have the following two inalienable and unlimitable 'rights': it cannot have its power removed or constrained by its subjects, and it cannot be charged with treating any of its subjects unjustly. Hobbes' justification of these 'rights' is that Leviathan embodies 'the will of the people', having been created by their mutual agreement in the interests of their own safety. Accordingly to oppose it would be self-contradictory: 'by this institution of a commonwealth, every particular man is author of all that the sovereign doth; and consequently he that complaineth of injury from his sovereign, complaineth of that whereof he himself is author; and therefore ought not to accuse any man but himself; no nor himself of injury; because to do injury to one's self is impossible.'[5]

For Hobbes 'the marks whereby a man may discern in what man, or assembly of men, the sovereign power is placed and resideth', are the authority to decide on war and peace, relations with other states, what can be published or practised in the commonwealth, property, punishments, official appointments, the distribution of honours, and all final matters at law. Hobbes identifies these powers as the 'essence of sovereignty'.[6]

Although the sovereign is above the law and unchallengeable, there is after all one constraint on it, arising from the very reason why it exists in the first place, namely to ensure its subjects' safety. Its 'office consisteth in the end, for which he was trusted with the sovereign power, namely the procuration of *the safety of the people*; to which he is obliged by the law of nature, and to render an account thereof to God, the author of that law, and to none but him'.[7] If Leviathan fails to do this, then because the overriding interest of the subjects is their self-preservation, they are entitled to disobey and even rebel. The right to self-preservation is not cancelled when all other freedoms are surrendered in establishing the original contract. In conceding this point Hobbes seems to plant a contradiction at the very heart of his thesis: for if the people ultimately have the right to overthrow Leviathan should it fail to protect them, they indeed have the ultimate say in the commonwealth.[8]

In the passage just quoted Hobbes invokes the concept of a 'law of nature' which binds Leviathan to guaranteeing the people's safety. The concept is ill-defined, and in supposedly providing the basis of Leviathan's duty to perform its part in the contract with the people, it is *ad hoc*. For if there is a natural law laying it down that the safety of individuals is the most important political consideration, why cannot this law be operative in the state of nature, governing people's behaviour there? Why can each individual not be 'obliged by the law of nature, and to render an account thereof to God, the author of that law, and to none but him', to ensure the safety of others as well as himself?

The concepts of natural law and natural rights are central in Locke's views also, but there they lead to quite different conclusions. For Locke the 'state of nature' was not a theatre of unending strife between individuals, but a place where they enjoyed freedom. Although most of that freedom was given up in exchange for the benefits of society, certain of them are inalienable: the rights to life, liberty and property. By this very fact it is impossible for absolute sovereignty to exist; for absolutism is inconsistent with the inalienable natural rights that people bring with them into the contract that creates society.

The concepts of natural law and natural rights are intimately connected. The latter consist in the fact that in the state of nature people are at complete liberty to use whatever nature affords in the way of food and shelter. Natural law is what identifies what is allowed given how things are in nature: 'all men are naturally in . . . a *state of perfect Freedom* to order their actions, and dispose of their Possessions, and Persons as they think fit, within the bounds of the Law of Nature, without asking leave, or depending on the Will of any other Man.'[9] This is because in the state of nature everyone is equal: because all men, says Locke, are 'furnished with like Faculties, sharing all in one Community of Nature, there cannot be supposed any such *Subordination* among us, that may authorize us to destroy one another, as if we were made for one another's uses, as the inferior ranks of Creatures are made for ours'.[10] Thus Locke rejects Filmer's claim that a hierarchy of status among men was established by God's grant of lordship to Adam in Eden, first over Eve, then over his sons, and thence onward to his successors.

Each person's right to self-preservation entails a correlative obligation on others to respect that right – indeed to go beyond that in being actively concerned for others' welfare in this regard. However, in the state of nature it is difficult to safeguard these

rights and to ensure the observance of the correlative obligations; Locke describes this as the 'inconvenience' of the state of
nature. But to institute a Hobbesian sovereign to overcome this
inconvenience would, he says, be worse than the inconvenience
itself, because nothing could stop an omnipotent sovereign
from preying on its subjects and even waging war on them.
Accordingly it is wrong in principle for people to give up their
rights to an absolute ruler; doing so would be not only to aban-
don the right to self-preservation but would make them unable
to perform their correlative duties to others.

> Freedom from Absolute, Arbitrary power is so necessary to, and
> closely joyned with a Man's Preservation, that he cannot part
> with it, but by what he forfeits his Preservation and Life together.
> For a Man, not having the Power of his own Life, cannot, by
> Compact, or his own Consent, *enslave himself* to any one, nor
> put himself under the Absolute, Arbitrary power of another, to
> take away his life, when he pleases. No body can give more
> Power than he has himself; and he that cannot take away his
> own Life, cannot give another power over it.[11]

In offering this argument against any form of absolutism,
Locke is premising an assumption that is independently questionable. In the passage just quoted he is suggesting that the
reason we cannot yield up the right of self-preservation is that
we do not own ourselves, but instead are owned by God, so our
freedom is not ours to give away. Locke thereby places humanity
under a theistic Leviathan, a doctrinally orthodox view, though
in reality a less appealing one even than Hobbes' view, for
whereas in Hobbes' view the very foundation of society is the
yielding of freedom to an earthly Leviathan, there is nevertheless the ultimately reserved right to rebel if Leviathan fails. If a

God of the type described in traditional religions exists, there would be no recourse against its tyranny.

If, however, we ignore the theological assumption behind Locke's view, it is the more persuasive. Civil society exists to protect individuals' lives, liberty and property. It is based on scrutable laws, with an independent judiciary to apply them, and agreed methods of enforcing them. And there the power of the state over the individual stops. 'Having in the State of Nature no Arbitrary Power over the Life, Liberty, or Possession of another', Locke wrote, 'but only so much as the Law of Nature gave him for the preservation of himself, and the rest of Mankind; this is all he doth, or can give up to the Commonwealth, and by it to the *Legislative Power*, so that the Legislative can have no more than this. Their Power in the utmost Bounds of it, is *limited to the publick good* of the Society.'[12] If a government acts in ways contrary to the 'publick good' it thereby renders itself illegitimate and accordingly 'dissolves' itself. This was the case with James II. Locke's point is clear: if a government fails in what it exists to perform, the people have not only the right but the duty to overthrow it, and replace it with a better.

A major reason why Locke's views were so influential in the American and French revolutions is that he introduced the idea of power as trusteeship, held by the consent – however bestowed – of those on whose behalf it is exercised. '*Who shall be Judge* whether the Prince or the Legislative act contrary to their trust?' Locke asked, and he answered, in a passage that has been seminal in the subsequent development of democratic ideas, '*The people shall be Judge*; for who shall be Judge whether his Trustee or Deputy acts well, and according to the Trust reposed in him, but he who deputes him, and must, by having deputed him have still a Power to discard him, when he fails in his Trust?'[13]

It came naturally to Locke to identify life, liberty and property as fundamental rights. In the parliamentary opposition between Presbyterians and Independents during the English Civil War these were the rights emphasized by the latter, and had Locke been an MP in that Parliament his loyalty would have lain with them. Each concept had a clear sense for him as for them. 'Liberty' meant the right of people to make their own choices in life. The right to property is a less obvious candidate for being taken as fundamental; Locke assumed so because, although land and what it provides is common property in the state of nature, he thought that when individuals mix their labour with parts of it, those parts come to be their private property, and no one else has a right to take away what their labour has appropriated.

In Locke's view, in the agreement that creates civil society ultimate power lies with the contracting parties, and they do not alienate but merely delegate it to the governing authority when the society-forming contract is made. If they are not satisfied with the exercise of it they can recall it. What the social contract creates is a *state*; he never uses the term 'sovereign' as Hobbes does; for Hobbes the contract empowers a sovereign absolutely, for Locke the contract does something quite different. For a 'state' and a 'government' are not at all the same thing. The state is the entity created by the contract; the government is the entity deputed to carry out the functions required for protecting the rights and enhancing the interests of citizens of the state.

Locke took it to be essential that the legislature (parliament) and executive (government of the day) should be separate. A legislature might be convened to make laws, and might then be dissolved until required again. But laws need to be applied and where necessary enforced, which is the executive's task. Locke said that these two organs of the state should not only be separate, but the people involved in them should be different also. If they were not, they 'may exempt themselves from the obedience to the Laws they make, and suit the Law, both in its making and its execution, to their own private Wish, and thereby come to have a distinct Interest from the rest of the Community, contrary to the end of Society and Government'.[14] This is yet another argument against absolute sovereignty, for an absolute sovereign is legislature and executive rolled into one omnipotent entity.

A crucial question is: when can it be said that a government has exceeded its authority, or failed in its duty? One has to allow that a government might occasionally err or make bad decisions, and one would not be for recalling governments at the drop of any old hat. But Locke thought the example of James II was completely clear: there was justification for depriving him of the throne because he had bypassed Parliament, made arbitrary laws, tried to reintroduce Roman Catholicism, and signed secret treaties with foreign powers, all in the interests of extending his own powers. This was a breach of faith with the people, whose only remedy was to rise against him.[15]

Locke is regarded as the founder of liberalism.[16] His views did not of course vanquish absolutism: Louis XIV, Frederick the Great in Prussia, Russia's Catherine the Great and all tsars since, Bolsheviks and Stalin, the Nazis, Maoists in China and elsewhere, Pol Pot, Pinochet, the absolute rulers in today's Middle East, Kim Jong-un, all testify that absolutism has continued to flourish.

As noted, Locke spoke of the 'consent of the people' without endorsing democracy as such. The word was still associated with Plato's condemnation; Hobbes was scathing about the Long Parliament in the England of his day, calling it 'democratical' as a term of abuse because he saw it as threatening to return society to the bloody state of nature. For him democracy meant nothing other than ochlocracy, anarchy perpetrated by ignorant, greedy and violent people.[17] Indeed the aims of Hobbes and Locke had very little to do with asserting anything like the idea that the populace of a state have a *right* to choose who shall govern them and in what way. The idea was remote from their thought. Hobbes' aim was to specify a regime that would ensure safety and order. Locke's aim was to defend the liberties and prerogatives of Parliament, which *a fortiori* provided protection to the citizen because Parliament's powers constituted a limitation on the Crown's powers, and to some degree instituted the principle of 'the rule of law not of man'.

Hobbes and Locke were not of course writing in a vacuum; Locke had Filmer as a useful overt springboard, and Hobbes as a secret one; while Hobbes was prompted in his thinking by Richard Hooker's *Ecclesiastical Polity* of 1593, in which the ideas both of a state of nature and a social contract figure. The ultimate source of the state of nature idea is the tradition derived from classical antiquity of a distantly past golden age in which people were wholly free and wholly autonomous. Where Hobbes saw the social compact as arising from people's concern to escape the bloody conditions of the war of all on all in that primitive state, Hooker saw it as arising from the consciousness of nature-dwelling people that their circumstances were attended by many practical inconveniences that would be overcome by living together in society. Locke's conception is closer to Hooker's.

But the key point about the idea of natural primordial liberty, some of which (Locke) or all of which (Hobbes) is yielded up for the advantages of living in society, is that the yielding up has as its reciprocal the promise of advantages. Because government consists, so to say, in the administration of the advantages, it exists by 'the will of the people' – to have what they have yielded all or part of their primordial liberty to get, to license the government to act on their behalf to supply it; in short: to perform the duty implicated in its half of the contract. In this indirect sense the acceptance of a regime of government is a passive expression of the consent deeply implicit in the social contract. 'The consent of the people' could be claimed by Locke and others at and in the period after his time without a single thought of democracy entering the equation. The kind of regime that was thus being conceived of is what has been described as *republican* rather than democratic.

The only seventeenth-century philosopher to think favourably of a form of democracy under its own name was Baruch Spinoza. He was just about to write the chapters on democracy in his *Tractatus Theologico-Politicus* when he died, but his discussion of two other types of regime, aristocracy and monarchy, contain enough for his views to be pieced together. Like his classical forebears he had a restricted view of who the enfranchised can be – namely, male citizens in good standing – for he excluded women, servants, foreigners, and unrespectable people. His grounds for championing democracy on this limited basis were of two kinds. One was that democracy recognizes the natural equality and freedom of men. The other, a more pragmatic reason, is that it is a better safeguard against arbitrary or absurd government. A democratic assembly is likely to arrive at better decisions than will a monarch or an aristocracy, he said, because in an assembly men will be more reasonable and well judging than if they are making decisions without a chance to 'have their wits sharpened by discussing, listening to others, and debating'.[18]

Spinoza defended freedom of thought and expression – which together entail freedom of religion also – and argued that it is a duty of government to protect them. He said he would give his support to any kind of regime that guaranteed this, though in his view a democracy would be most likely to do it. His idea of the consent of the people, as with Locke and Hobbes (who in *Behemoth* wrote 'the power of the mighty hath no foundation but in the opinion and belief of the people'[19]) – was not one that required voting, for it lay in the demonstration of the people's willingness, or at least lack of express unwillingness, to go along with the arrangements for government under which they lived. In Locke the notion in play is 'tacit consent'; by living in the state and observing its laws and rules an individual tacitly consents to its government. Hobbes saw a rather different angle to this, expressed in his observation that 'the reputation of power is power'[20] – that is, if a person or institution is believed to possess power, he or it will therefore in fact possess it. Once that belief ceases, power ceases with it: think of the Wizard of Oz discovered behind his curtain.

By the end of the seventeenth century both thought and practice regarding the source of political authority in a state were at a fork in the road. The France of Louis XIV, then at its historical zenith, and Prussia and Russia in the eighteenth century, reaffirmed by their very existence the principle of monarchical absolutism. It was not until the close of the First World War that the principle at last faltered; that was when rule by emperors in Russia and Austro-Hungary ended, although in the latter case some constitutional change limiting the Crown's power had been occasioned by the events of 1848. The collapse of monarchical rule in Russia was replaced by equally authoritarian Bolshevik and then Stalinist rule, so the tide of history cannot be said to have completely set in a democratic direction as a result of the activism of Levellers or, more significantly, the writings of Spinoza and especially Locke.[21] However, the changes they wrought in thought about these matters was influential in the following century's Enlightenment and the historical revolutions that occurred at its end. For it was in these events that a solution to the dilemma of democracy began to emerge in ways anticipating contemporary representative democracy.

4

THE BEGINNINGS OF A
SOLUTION PART II

Montesquieu, Rousseau

Although all the thinkers of the seventeenth century other than
Spinoza shied away from using the term 'democracy' in other
than a pejorative sense, those of the eighteenth century were
less fastidious, being prepared to consider the conditions under
which democracy might not merely be possible but even desirable. The two of most note are Montesquieu and Rousseau.
Their reasons for being sceptical about the possibility of democracy are instructive, not least because the first of them inferred
from his discussion both of it and of other forms of government
an idea that was adopted in practice by the makers of the
American constitution later in the century, namely the checks
and balances of a system of separated powers.

Montesquieu's aim in his classic *The Spirit of the Laws* (1748)
was to examine the nature of law and government and to urge
that they be made conformable to the factors that he saw as the
appropriate influences on them, namely the geography, climate,
customs, occupations, historical antecedents, and character of

the people in relation to which and to whom they exist. As this suggests, his aim was not merely descriptive but prescriptive, applying the lessons of history to illustrate how such conformability or lack of it worked and should work in practice.

In Montesquieu's classification of forms of government there are two types of republican government, democratic and aristocratic, and two other types, monarchical and despotic, distinguished by the fact that a monarch does, whereas a despot does not, rule according to laws that are 'fixed and established'. Despotism thus resides in the arbitrariness of the ruler's will or whim.

In defining a democracy as a system in which sovereignty lies with the people (for suitable 'the people') Montesquieu was employing a standard view of what the concept meant in classical antiquity. But as with all who thought democracy only possible in ideal circumstances, he identified 'the principle of democracy' as *virtue*, meaning that 'the person entrusted with the execution of the laws is sensible of his being subject to their direction', for when laws are suspended or disobeyed 'the state is certainly undone'.[1]

This is what he thought had happened in the English Civil War:

> A very droll spectacle it was in the last century to behold the impotent efforts of the English towards the establishment of democracy. As they who had a share in the direction of public affairs were void of virtue; as their ambition was inflamed by the success of the most daring of their members; as the prevailing parties were successively animated by the spirit of faction, the government was continually changing: the people, amazed at so many revolutions, in vain attempted to erect a commonwealth. At length, when the country had undergone the most violent

shocks, they were obliged to have recourse to the very government which they had so wantonly proscribed.[2]

It might seem that Montesquieu's talk of virtue must really be
something more specific than is usually meant in the moral
sense, perhaps 'political virtue' given that he defines it in one
place as obedience to the law. He elsewhere suggests that virtue
is love of country or love of equality. The equation between
patriotism and equality is not immediately obvious, but a little
reflection suggests that he means that to love your country is to
love your fellows, which in turn is to think of you and your
fellows as equals. This would protect against 'faction', that is,
party divisions and animosity.

The 'principles' of monarchy and despotism – namely what
keep them going – are respectively honour and fear. What
keeps democracy going is the far more demanding matter of 'a
constant preference of public to private interest . . . [it] limits
ambition to the sole desire, to the sole happiness, of doing greater
services to our country than the rest of our fellow citizens . . . a
self-renunciation, which is ever arduous and painful'.[3] This is one
main reason why democracy does not work, Montesquieu is
suggesting, because people are not that selfless.

The comparison Montesquieu draws is with monastic life,
where personal desires are subordinated to the rule under which
monks live; the more strictly the rule governs them, the more
desirous they are of obeying it. To achieve such an attitude and
practice of self-renunciation a democracy must bring 'the whole
power of education' to bear on its citizens so that they can focus
their ambitions entirely on the good of the country. The law
should impose frugality, to prevent individuals from seeking
private instead of public gain, and for the same reason property
should be equitably distributed. The best circumstance for a

democracy to flourish in these circumstances is for the country and its population to be small.

As the passage about the Levellers' failed efforts in the English Civil War shows, Montesquieu thought that there are two chief ways in which democracy fails. One is the spirit of extreme equality, the other is the spirit of inequality. The latter arises when citizens cease to identify their country's good as greater than their private good, with the result that they work at advancing their own interests at the expense of those of their fellows. An aspect of this is the desire of individuals to acquire more power than their fellow citizens, in order to direct matters in accordance with their own desires. When groups of individuals get together to achieve this for themselves as a group, the result is factionalism, the formation of political parties.

The former, the spirit of extreme equality, arises when the people cease to respect the ministers and magistrates they have elected, and refuse to obey them, wishing instead 'to manage everything for themselves, to debate for the senate, to execute for the magistrate, to decide for the judges'.[4] This is anarchy, and anarchic situations are ripe for hijacking by despotism.

One of the great deficits of despotism, obviously, is the loss of liberty, which Montesquieu is careful to distinguish from licence to do as one pleases; we have liberty, he says, when we live under laws that protect us while leaving us free to do what we wish as long as we do not harm or interfere with others. To ensure liberty the government must be structured to guard against what would deprive us of it. 'Experience shows that every man invested with power is apt to abuse it', Montesquieu says, and therefore 'it is necessary from the very nature of things that power should be a check to power'.[5] This is effected by keeping separate the legislative, executive and judicial arms of government. If they are mutually independent they will counterbalance each other, but if they are in the same hands there is no safeguard against possible tyranny.

The legislature should be bicameral, each of the houses having the power to block laws proposed by the other house. The legislature alone should have the power to raise taxes, which means it can starve the executive of resources if it disapproves of what it is doing. Reciprocally, the executive should have the power to veto legislation proposed by the legislature. And finally, the judiciary should be independent of both the other arms, restricting itself to monitoring application of the law in specific cases in a consistent and transparent way.

This structure was adopted by the founders of America after the revolution of 1776. It is a magnificent structure in theory. In practice matters are rather different. It transpires that unless there is a considerable degree of consensus between the Houses of Congress and between them and the Presidency, partial or complete paralysis of the system occurs. During the two presidential terms of Barack Obama the entire country was more than once threatened with standstill by the inability of the three branches to agree a budget. As party rivalry between Republicans and Democrats sharpened in the second half of the twentieth century, the in-built sclerosis of the system became more apparent. Moreover the practice of appointing Supreme Court justices for life on party lines results in veering interpretations of the Constitution and the laws between liberal and conservative readings, on occasion dependent on the retirement or death of a single member of the Court.

John Stuart Mill noted the risk of deadlock and inefficiency in the arrangement proposed by Montesquieu and chosen by America. For him as for other commentators such as Harold Laski, separation of powers too easily degenerates into confusion of functions. Where the legislative and executive functions are in the same hands, said Laski, there is both harmony and efficiency, which is why for a good part of the history of the United States there has been a *de facto* combination of powers with legislature and executive – Congress and President – working together when the same party has control of both branches.

Ironically, Montesquieu's suggestions about separation of powers was based on his experience of England, where he had lived for two years before embarking on the *Laws*. The Houses of Commons and Lords, the Crown, and the independent judiciary provided his model. But he was mistaken in his reading of them. Because the executive is drawn from the majority party in the legislature, and because the Crown and two Houses constitute the single entity 'the Crown in Parliament', the result is that there is no separation of powers at all. Executive and legislature are one. Moreover the judiciary did not have the power to strike down laws enacted by Parliament, and to this day still cannot, though if legislation is inconsistent with the Human Rights Act 2000 it can ask Parliament to look at the law again with a view to making it consistent. The power of striking down laws as unconstitutional requires a clear constitution – preferable, by far, is a written one such as the United States has. The United Kingdom's constitution has been aptly described as 'a set of understandings which no one understands'. The standard objection to written constitutions – inflexibility – is a calumny on the common sense of humankind: why cannot a constitution be written which allows that things change, and that there should be rational and careful procedures for adjusting in line with them?

The second figure who looms in eighteenth-century thought about democracy is Jean-Jacques Rousseau. From a nostalgic memory of simple face-to-face communities in the Swiss cantons, where all the adult males knew one another and jointly performed the offices of local government as if they constituted an ideal version of a classical city state, Rousseau derived the idea of completely harmonious interests in which the will of each individual is in conformity with the 'general will': 'When we see among the happiest people in the world bands of peasants regulating the affairs of state under an oak tree, and always acting wisely, can we help feeling a certain contempt for the refinements of other nations, which employ so much skill and effort to make themselves at once illustrious and wretched?' he asks, and adds, of the peasants under their oak tree: 'A state thus governed needs very few laws.'[6]

Rousseau's notion of the 'general will' is not entirely perspicuous, but has these features: it is distinct from the idea of the will of the majority, or the sum of what all individuals will, but instead can be described as the will of a whole society treated as an organism. The law expresses the general will, which people therefore obey even when they are punished by it. The desire individuals have to be good is expressed as a desire to obey the general will, because the general will embodies wisdom and virtue in excess of what any individual could embody. To act contrary to the general will is accordingly to act against one's own true interests and desires, if only one understood what they are. But we do not often know what our real interests are; individual wills are corrupted by the sophistications of society.

Because the general will is supremely good, Rousseau said, a state would be justified in compelling people to act in conformity with it. This point has roused the opposition of many commentators since, seeing totalitarian implications in it, especially given its vulnerability to exploitation by demagogues and dictators claiming to know what the general will is even if no one else does. Generally speaking, when politicians claim to know or be acting on behalf of 'the will of the people' one should be reaching for a thousand-litre tank of scepticism – yet 'the general will' is even more than the 'will of the people' in that it is their will whether they know it or not: a dangerous conception.

Nevertheless, a state in which the will of each individual accorded perfectly with the general will, in circumstances similar to those enjoyed by the peasants under their oak tree, would be a democracy. As a matter of practicality Rousseau was sceptical that democracy as thus 'strictly understood' was possible. It would only be possible in a small society where everyone participated, or in larger societies where the opposite would be necessary – that is, if people could deliberate in private once they are properly informed, free from persuasion or influence by others. In this case, he said, it is 'essential, if the general will is to make itself known, that there should be no partial society in the state, and that each citizen should express only his own opinion'.[7] But as soon as groupings form, as they inevitably do, or people fall under the influence of orators, the aggregate of their individual votes no longer expresses the general will. Factions, intrigues and parties arise, so that there are no longer 'as many votes as there are men, but only as many as there are associations'.[8]

Accordingly, 'if we take the term in the strict sense', he said, 'there never has been a real democracy, and there never will be.'[9] An obvious reason is that the people cannot remain in permanent assembly to manage public affairs, so they will delegate to various tribunals, one of which will sooner or later acquire more authority than the others, thus taking power into its own hands. The inevitability of this, and the yet more significant reason that the conditions in which alone a democracy can exist – in a very small state in which the people are simple, frugal and equal – are unlikely ever to be found in the world as it is, together explain why democracy is impossible. 'Were there a people of gods', Rousseau wrote, 'their government would be democratic. So perfect a government is not for men.'

These points in fact reprise, in a different key, the recurrent and persistent theme that pure or direct democracy is impossible because of its unsustainability given human psychology and the human condition. Critics of the overtly Platonic kind argue that by its very nature unqualified democracy is apt to degenerate into a far less desirable form of government even than those thought to be higher up the scale of regime types – in Plato's ascending list oligarchy, timocracy and aristocracy. Here and in the arguments of most of Plato's fellow anti-democrats the blame is placed on people and the effects of their behaviour on social organization. Rousseau's way of putting the matter is that the fault lies with the corruption and complexity of society and their effects on behaviour.

Rousseau's talk of the 'general will', if not the concept as he himself actually meant it, passed into the rhetoric of politics very rapidly. Article 6 of the French Revolution's Declaration of the Rights of Man and the Citizen says: 'The law is the expression of the general will. All citizens have the right to contribute personally, or through their representatives, to its formation. It must be the same for all, whether it protects or punishes.' It also lies behind Article 3: 'The principle of any sovereignty resides essentially in the Nation. No body, no individual can exert authority which does not emanate expressly from it.' It was taken to be an encapsulation of the principle that the only source there can be of political authority is 'the will of the people', the fundamental principle of democracy. That the two ideas – democracy and 'the will of the people' – are different was not noticed: rhetoric is not about distinctions but persuasion.

5

SOLUTIONS PROPOSED PART I

Madison, Constant

In June 1776 the American state of Virginia adopted a 'Declaration of Rights' whose first three articles read as follows:

> Section 1. That all men are by nature equally free and independent and have certain inherent rights, of which, when they enter into a state of society, they cannot, by any compact, deprive or divest their posterity; namely the enjoyment of life and liberty, with the means of acquiring and possessing property, and pursuing and obtaining happiness and safety. [One will recognize the direct influence of Locke in these words.] Section 2. That all power is vested in, and consequently derived from, the people; that magistrates are their trustees and servants and at all times amenable to them. Section 3. That government is, or ought to be, instituted for the common benefit, protection, and security of the people, nation, or community . . . when any government shall be found inadequate or contrary to these purposes, a majority of the community has an indubitable, inalienable, and

indefeasible right to reform, alter, or abolish it, in such manner as shall be judged most conducive to the public weal. [Locke again.][1]

The Declaration was not the state's constitution. A formal constitution was adopted seventeen days later, setting out more detailed matters such as, among other things, the legislative structure and electoral arrangements. The Declaration was added to the Constitution more than half a century later, in 1830, by which time it had already begun to make difficulties for the state – partly because of the clash between the principles it embodied and the actual constitutional arrangements for the state's government, and partly because of certain ambiguities it implied; for example, when the southern states seceded from the Union in 1860, precipitating the American Civil War, Virginia was split between the two sides in the conflict because its western counties believed that the Declaration mandated a referendum on secession, which the state government refused to hold.

The most significant impact of the Declaration was in its contemporary reception. It influenced Thomas Jefferson in writing the United States Declaration of Independence in that same month of June 1776, it influenced John Adams in writing the constitution of Massachusetts in 1780, and it influenced James Madison in writing the Bill of Rights in 1789.

The opening of Jefferson's Declaration of Independence is close in wording to the Virginia Declaration:

We hold these truths to be self-evident, that all men are created equal, that they are endowed by their Creator with certain unal-ienable Rights, that among these are Life, Liberty and the Pursuit of Happiness. That to secure these rights, Governments are instituted among Men, deriving their just powers from the consent of the governed. That whenever any Form of Government becomes destructive of these ends, it is the Right of the People to alter or to abolish it, and to institute new Government, laying its foundation on such principles and organizing its powers in such form, as to them shall seem most likely to effect their Safety and Happiness.[2]

The first thing to note is that whereas the Virginia Declaration affirms that 'all power is vested in, and consequently derived from, the people' and that 'when any government shall be found inadequate or contrary to these purposes, a majority of the community has an indubitable, inalienable, and indefeasible right to reform, alter, or abolish it', the state's constitution adopted less than three weeks later was not nearly so democratic. It gave the vote only to men of property and wealth: it was a classic timocracy. Efforts to reduce the property qualification were resisted by those who held it until seventy years later, in 1851, and accordingly the state was run by the rich landowners of the relatively unpopulated eastern regions while the more populous and poorer western regions – those that eventually broke away to form West Virginia in the Civil War – were underrepresented.

Of course, the wording in both the Virginia and Independence Declarations was aimed at justifying repudiation of the authority of George III in London, rather than setting up genuine democracy in America. The equality of man was about the colonial rebels' refusal to bend the knee to a far-off king, not about the equality of black men and white men at home. The right to throw off an unjust government was a justification for rebellion against George III, not a commitment to rule by the people. Most crucially, 'the people' were not the populace, but that section of it which had the vote and therefore held the power. The enfranchised called themselves 'the representatives of the people', just as in the English Bill of Rights in which 'Lords Spiritual and Temporal' were included among the 'representatives of the people', paternalistically acting on their behalf. It was as natural to the drafters of the English Bill of Rights to think of lords representing the people by right of superior status endowed by heredity, office or wealth, as it was for the members of the Virginia Convention to think that the right to vote lay with those who had the most material interest in the wellbeing of the state, viz. men of property. James Harrington and Henry Ireton and a long tradition before both gave the Virginians their justification for so thinking.

There is a striking difference between Jefferson's words and those of the Virginia Declaration's drafter, George Mason. It lies in the former's choice of the word 'consent' rather than the latter's quite unequivocal statement, 'all power is vested in, and consequently derived from, the people', words which Jefferson had before his eyes as he wrote his own version. He substituted a much less radical idea: 'Governments . . . [derive] their just powers from the consent of the governed.' Where Mason had thought bottom-up from the people to what they authorized, Jefferson thought top-down from government to what gave them their authority; and the difference is not merely one of phraseology. In Mason's view the people had to voice their grant of power to government. Jefferson's view leaves room for saying that the consent of the governed could be manifested in ways other than voting – by tacit agreement or passive acceptance, for example.

Between the Virginia Declaration and the Virginia Constitution of 1776, and between the Virginia Declaration and the Declaration of Independence, all three documents written in the selfsame month, the shadow of Platonic concern falls, just as it had done in Putney between the 'Agreement of the People' and the caution of Ireton and Cromwell that prompted them to argue for a property-based franchise. The crucial point in every case was the dilemma of deriving authority for government from the people, without making the people the government – that is, in the view of those to whom the Platonic concerns vividly impressed themselves: without making the unorganized, uninformed, emotionally motivated, often prejudiced and sometimes intemperate people the government. Jefferson's 'consent of the governed' is accordingly the same as Sir William Temple's 'consent of the people'; it lies in the agreement, the acceptance, of the regime of government, though passively and tacitly manifested; the organs and activities of government are insulated by the indirectness of the route by which the authority of this consent reaches them.

George Mason had drawn both on England's 1668 Bill of Rights and on Locke's writings when drafting the Virginia Declaration, but he went considerably further than either. Indeed he reached back to Putney, if not indeed all the way to Pericles. But as the first document in America addressing constitutional matters, the scope it gave to citizens' rights and their role in authorizing government did not chime with the views of Mason's contemporaries. They were too well read in Plato and Aristotle, and in Roman history, to wish to follow him into so unequivocal an endorsement of democracy. James Madison described democracy as 'the most vile form of government . . . democracies have ever been spectacles of turbulence and contention; have ever been found incompatible with personal security or the rights of property, and have in general been as short in their lives as they have been violent in their deaths.'[3] The second President of the United States, John Adams, thought likewise: 'Democracy never lasts long. It soon wastes, exhausts and murders itself. There never was a democracy yet that did not commit suicide.'[4]

As a result the founders of the United States took their lesson from Montesquieu instead, and designed the mixed constitution of checks and balances intended to ensure that although the 'consent of the people' would be sought as part of the authorizing basis for government, the institutions of government would be a combination of elected, indirectly elected and appointed bodies that between them would 'refine and enlarge the public views',[5] in effect filtering out the self-interest, lack of information, short-termism and prejudice of the many. The idea is one that, as close as possible without actually saying so, frankly applies the advice of classical antiquity: that government must be in the hands of those competent for the job – viz. an elite. In rejecting the idea that an elite either of property or heredity should rule, Mason had rejected this idea; his contemporaries enshrined it in the Constitution.

What the founders were working out was a conception of political authority which has been called *republican* rather than *democratic*, in making the 'consent of the people', even if expressed at the ballot box on a wide suffrage, just one aspect of the structure designed to produce sound and stable government. Mason's overenthusiasm aside, it was the Virginian ideas of Jefferson and Madison that underlay this republicanism, sometimes called 'Jeffersonian democracy' to distinguish it from the more populist 'Jacksonian democracy' that arrived with President Andrew Jackson fifty years later.

The structure set up from the beginning in the new state was (and to a large extent still remains) as follows. The lower of the two Houses of Congress, the House of Representatives, is directly elected. Until the passing of the 17th Amendment in

1913 senators were appointed by state legislatures; the amendment provided that each state would send two directly elected senators to Washington, no matter how populous the state. Accordingly a non-proportionality persists to protect the interests of less populous states. The President is elected by an Electoral College whose members are delegated from the states proportionally to the popular vote in each, the losing candidate sometimes having a larger popular vote than the winning candidate therefore. Not until the passage of the 19th Amendment in 1920 were women given the vote. The 15th Amendment gave African-American males the vote in 1870, but in the southern states Jim Crow laws and other discriminatory practices erected various barriers denying it to them until the Voting Rights Act of 1965 remedied the situation.

In the Jackson era after 1828, which broke what had been the monopoly of Virginia and Massachusetts on the White House – Jackson was a populist figure from Tennessee – the franchise was progressively extended to more and more white males, until eventually all property and wealth qualifications for the franchise were abolished, the last of them in North Carolina in 1856.

As this sketch shows, only the House of Representatives is directly elected (on a first-past-the-post – FPTP – system). The fact that each state sends two senators to Washington irrespective of absolute size of the electorates involved, and the fact that the President is elected by an Electoral College which does not always reflect the popular vote, indicates that a significant degree of non-proportionality is built into the system. And finally one recalls that the Supreme Court, playing a highly significant constitutional role with great social and political implications, is appointed not elected. Of the four arms of state therefore, three are in the distal half of a scale beginning with direct democracy, and the fourth is not all that close to this origin on the scale, because the FPTP system effectively disenfranchises every voter whose vote does not go to the winner (see pp. 138–9).

The constitutional settlement of the new United States evidently took fully to heart the strictures levelled at democracy by almost every thinker from Plato to its own day. The question is whether this solution to the dilemma – the dilemma of how the consent, authorization or agreement of the enfranchised can be taken as granted in a system whose structures as it were pasteurize it (some would say: castrate it) – is defensible.

James Madison, in one of the most cited of the *Federalist Papers*, No. 10, argued in favour of this principle as follows. For Madison a great danger to sound government and the stability of the state is factionalism, which he saw as an inherent vice of 'popular government'. It is desirable therefore to have a system which protects against the effects of factionalism – the 'instability, injustice, and confusion' it introduces into public councils – without impugning the principle of popular consent. 'Complaints are everywhere heard', Madison wrote, 'that the public good is disregarded in the conflicts of rival parties, and that measures are too often decided, not according to the rules of justice and the rights of the minor party, but by the superior force of an interested and overbearing majority.'[6]

By 'faction' Madison meant a political party or movement: 'By a faction, I understand a number of citizens, whether amounting to a majority or a minority of the whole, who are united and actuated by some common impulse of passion, or of interest, adversed to the rights of other citizens, or to the permanent and aggregate interests of the community.'[7] He saw two ways of 'curing the mischiefs' of factionalism, one directed at its causes, the other at its effects.

To remove the causes of factionalism there are likewise two options. Either one denies everyone the liberty that gives rise to it, or one somehow makes everyone think alike so that they will not disagree. Neither is practicable. 'Liberty is to faction what air is to fire, an aliment without which it instantly expires. But it could not be less folly to abolish liberty, which is essential to political life, because it nourishes faction, than it would be to wish the annihilation of air, which is essential to animal life, because it imparts to fire its destructive agency.'[8] The second option is impracticable because human reason is fallible and so long as people are free to think they will do so in ways that differ from each other. Moreover the differences between people will result in inequalities, not least in property – the more energetic and enterprising will accumulate more property than the less enterprising, and thereby another source of division into competing interest groups arises.

Thus 'the latent causes of faction are sown into the nature of man . . . So strong is this propensity of mankind to fall into mutual animosities, that where no substantial occasion presents itself, the most frivolous and fanciful distinctions have been sufficient to kindle their unfriendly passions and excite their most violent conflicts',[9] as for example the differences of religious opinion.

But it is the difference in property that is the primary cause of factionalism. Such differences are inevitable. 'A landed interest, a manufacturing interest, a mercantile interest, a moneyed interest, with many lesser interests, grow up of necessity in civilized nations, and divide them into different classes, actuated by different sentiments and views.'[10] No one is allowed to sit as a judge in his own cause, because he would naturally be biased in his own favour; yet a legislative assembly, whose acts are in effect 'so many judicial determinations', is made up of people whose personal interests are engaged in the legislation.

What are the different classes of legislators but advocates and parties to the causes which they determine? Is a law proposed concerning private debts? It is a question to which the creditors are parties on one side and the debtors on the other. Justice ought to hold the balance between them. Yet the parties are, and must be, themselves the judges; and the most numerous party, or, in other words, the most powerful faction must be expected to prevail. Shall domestic manufactures be encouraged, and in what degree, by restrictions on foreign manufactures? are questions which would be differently decided by the landed and the manufacturing classes, and probably by neither with a sole regard to justice and the public good.[11]

Madison rejects a solution akin to Plato's idea in *Republic* Book VI for a disinterested philosopher king, namely 'the enlightened statesman'[12] who can adjudicate between competing interests, on the ground that there can be no guarantee that such a figure will always be available. This exhausts the possibilities of managing the problem from the side of its causes. The alternative therefore is to mitigate its effects.

An interest can always of course be checked if it has minority support in a populace; the real problem, says Madison, is when the majority of the people wishes to impose its interest on others, even in opposition to the good of the state as a whole. To protect against this the majority must 'be rendered, by their number and local situation, unable to concert and carry into effect schemes of oppression'. Otherwise:

A common passion or interest will, in almost every case, be felt by a majority of the whole; a communication and concert result from the form of government itself; and there is nothing to check the inducements to sacrifice the weaker party or an obnoxious individual. Hence it is that such democracies have ever been spectacles of turbulence and contention; have ever been found incompatible with personal security or the rights of property; and have in general been as short in their lives as they have been violent in their deaths.[13]

Accordingly Madison proposes a *republic* as the 'cure' for this problem. In his meaning of the term, a republic is a political order in which government is delegated to a small number of citizens elected by the rest. This will 'refine and enlarge the public views, by passing them through the medium of a chosen body of citizens, whose wisdom may best discern the true interest of the country, and whose patriotism and love of justice will be least likely to sacrifice it to temporary or partial considerations.' Of course the government might still fall into the hands of people who are not wise, patriotic and just, but instead have only their own interests at heart; but this is less likely to happen in a large state than in a small one. So the desideratum is to have a large and populous republic. Among other things this will ensure that unworthy candidates will be less able to practise the arts of demagoguery on the electorate, because the electorate will be too large for all of it to be fooled at the same time. And whereas in a small country it is easy for a majority party to form, in a large one there are too many diverse interests for this to happen so easily.

This argument sets out the grounds for indirect democracy in preference to forms of democracy that could 'sacrifice the weaker party or an obnoxious individual'. It is not Plato's argument against democracy, because it does not invoke the spectre of the mob, and it accepts the principle of the 'consent of the people'. But it offers a remedy against the problem Madison identified as more likely – the tyranny of the majority over minorities and individuals. That is what factionalism can too easily cause. His remedy – the institutional filters that render democracy indirect – is such as to raise a question mark over de Tocqueville's claim in the second volume of *Democracy in America* that 'it is really the people who lead, and, although the form of the government is representative, clearly the opinions, prejudices, interests, and even the passions of the people cannot encounter any lasting obstacles that can prevent them from appearing in the daily leadership of society'. In a republic as envisaged by Madison, it is precisely not the people who lead; they give consent to leadership, which is for him the better point.

Alexander Hamilton, another of the *Federalist Papers* authors, concurred. In *Federalist Papers* No. 73 he wrote that the institutional checks designed into the structure of government would prevent 'excess of lawmaking' and would 'keep things in the same state in which they happen to be at any given period . . . the injury which possibly may be done by defeating a few good laws will be amply compensated by preventing a number of bad ones'.

Events occurring not long after Madison and Hamilton wrote suggest, however, that they were premature in restricting anxiety just to the dangers of unqualified majoritarianism. The events were the Terror into which revolutionary France's democratic experiment collapsed in 1793–4; they and the same anxieties Madison felt prompted Benjamin Constant and John Stuart Mill to think about the added problem of the inconsistency of majoritarianism with liberty.

Looked at from a bird's-eye view, the transitions in France's constitutional arrangements from the day that the Third Estate occupied the king's Tennis Court on 20 June 1789 until the day that Napoleon Bonaparte declared himself emperor on 18 May

1804 – fifteen long, tumultuous and bloody years later, and still a decade from the end of the wars thus precipitated – are a laboratory of all the theories and fears of those who, from the fifth century BCE onwards, had given thought to the matter of government. The familiar lessons were taught. Revolutions are not often inherited by those who begin them; they far too often end in dictatorships or circumstances little different from those that precipitated them. Plato's taxonomy of the stages that lead into and out of democracy applies in rough approximation here, for the tumults and changes in France from 1789 until the Terror, through the attempted government of the *Corps législatif* with its Council of Five Hundred and Council of Ancients and Directory, until the Napoleonic era of Consulship and then Empire, are: monarchy to democracy to ochlocracy to dictatorship.

In the process many noble and worthwhile sentiments were expressed, not least in the Declaration of the Rights of Man and the Citizen whose aspirations are unarguably fine, and in the effects of Napoleon's rule, with the liberation of Europe's Jewish populations from civil disabilities and the spread of ideas in the Code Napoleon; so the simplistic division into 'all good' and 'all bad' does not apply to the story as a whole. But it certainly applies to the Terror, a tremendous example – in all senses of this adjective – of ochlocracy in action. The guillotine, a merciful machine if judicial murder has to be enacted, was not the only despatcher of the many thousands who died in that blood-soaked period; mobs killed without trial, many of the victims were innocent of anything other than the jealousy or spite of neighbours, the checks imposed on behaviour by morality and law were trampled underfoot.

Historians agree that the military reverses of 1792 and 1793 boosted support for the more radical elements in the Revolution, the Montagnards, the favourites of Paris's *sans culottes*. In July 1793 the Montagnards seized control of affairs from the more moderate Girondins and set in place a radical social and economic policy, controlling prices, distributing welfare to the poor, making education free and compulsory, and confiscating and selling the property of emigrés to raise money. These are legitimate initiatives for a left-wing programme, but the reaction they provoked – uprisings of protest all round the country, in the Vendée, Normandy, Provence, Brittany, in Lyon and Bordeaux – were met with a ferocious response in the form of the Terror. Of the three hundred thousand people who were arrested in the Terror, only some seventeen thousand were tried and executed under a form of judicial process; the unnumbered victims besides were arbitrarily despatched. Liberated into licence, mobs were ruler, judge, jury, and executioner rolled into one. And as almost inevitably happens, the sponsor of the Terror, 'Incorruptible' Robespierre, was himself executed the day after he fell from power, 27 July 1794.

Benjamin Constant drew a stark lesson from these events: that unqualified democracy is a threat to liberty. In his view a failure to distinguish between two kinds of liberty – ancient and modern – caused many of the evils of the French Revolution. The difference lies in the forms of government of the ancients and moderns, the latter having representative government and the former not. 'Representative government is a *modern* discovery', wrote Constant, 'and you will see that the condition of the human race in antiquity made it impossible then for such an institution to be introduced or established. The ancient peoples couldn't feel the need for it, or appreciate its advantages. Their social organization led them to want a kind of freedom totally different from what representative government grants to us.'[14]

For a modern, said Constant, the word 'liberty' connotes the right to be subject only to laws, and to a non-arbitrary due process of their application; the rights to freedom of expression, freedom to choose one's employment, and freedom to use and dispose of one's own property; the right to come and go as one pleases, without having to explain to anyone what one is doing, and to use one's time in one's own chosen way; the right to associate with others of one's choice; and the right 'to have some influence on the administration of the government – by electing all or some of its officials, or through representations, petitions, or demands that the authorities are more or less obliged to take into consideration.'[15]

To the ancients, by contrast, the idea of liberty was the idea of 'carrying out *collectively but directly* many parts of the over-all functions of government',[16] by congregating in the public square to debate and decide about peace, war and alliances; to debate and vote on laws; to pronounce judgments in legal cases; and to summon and examine those appointed to carry out the work of government.

But, said Constant, though the ancients called this 'liberty', they saw no conflict between it and the complete subjection of individuals to social authority in all matters of private life.[17]

All private actions were strictly monitored. No room was allowed for individual independence of opinions, or of choice of work, or—especially—of religion. We moderns regard the right to choose one's own religious affiliation as one of the most precious, but to the ancients this would have seemed criminal and sacrilegious. In all the matters that seem to us the most important, the authority of the collective interposed itself and obstructed the will of individuals. The Spartan Therpandrus can't add a string to his lyre without offending the magistrates. In the most domestic of relations the public authority again intervenes: a young Spartan isn't free to visit his new bride whenever he wants to. In Rome, the searching eye of the censors penetrate into family life. The laws regulate *mœurs*, and as *mœurs* touch on everything, there's nothing that the laws don't regulate.[18]

Thus among the ancients, people (more accurately: adult male citizens) are sovereign in public affairs and slaves in private affairs. 'As a member of the collective body he interrogates, dismisses, condemns, impoverishes, exiles or sentences to death his magistrates and superiors; as a subject of the collective body he can himself be deprived of his status, stripped of his privileges, banished, put to death, by the free choice of the whole of which he is a part.'[19]

For the moderns matters are exactly the other way round. Things could be as they were in ancient times because states were small and unpopulous. In modern times states are large and populous. This great difference explains for Constant how the concept of liberty came to be misapplied in the French Revolution. 'The aim of our reformers in the French Revolution was noble and generous' because they sought to overthrow a system of government that was harsh, repressive, absurd in principle, and wretched in action because the final decision lay with a single individual, the monarch. But the reformers were working with the ideas of two philosophers who had not taken into account the significance of the changes that had occurred in society since ancient times. These were Rousseau and the Abbé de Mably.

Both thought that 'the authority of the social body is liberty', and that 'any means seemed good if it extended the active scope of that authority over the recalcitrant part of human existence whose independence they deplored.'[20] The leaders of the French

Revolution were inspired by this idea, and sought to carry it out by applying the power they had seized: 'They believed that everything should give way before the collective will, and that all restrictions on individual rights would be amply compensated for by participation in social power.' Constant then drily adds, 'You know what came of this.'[21]

In a version of Plato's view that ochlocracy must soon cede to tyranny because disorder becomes intolerably burdensome and people welcome the return of order that a tyrant imposes, Constant argued that the burden of private bondage in the service of public liberty comes to seem more onerous than the public bondage but private liberty experienced under a tyrant.

But of course, the desired aim is a conjunction of both kinds of liberty, public and private. 'It is necessary', wrote Constant, 'for us to learn to combine the two.'

To this point it is impossible to disagree with him: but the dilemma returns in the very next words – the concluding words – of his famous essay.

The work of the legislator is not complete when he has simply brought peace to the people. Even when the populace is satisfied, there is much left to do. Institutions must carry out the moral education of the citizens. By respecting their individual rights, securing their independence, refraining from troubling their work, institutions must nevertheless dedicate themselves to influencing public affairs, calling on the people to contribute to the exercise of power through their decisions and their votes, guaranteeing their right of control and supervision through the expression of their opinions, and by shaping them up through the exercise of these high functions, give them both the desire and the power to perform them.[22]

In these words a fudge occurs: 'the people' have to be educated to be suitable to exercise the 'control and supervision' of the legislators and institutions who have to 'carry out the moral education of the citizens' and protect, guide and influence them. So, who in this game of ping pong is taking the lead? The trope of the 'demos suitable for democracy' and the trope of 'institutions designed to filter the will of the people into good government' are here both in play, compounding rather than resolving the problem given that in other thinkers one or other of these resolving options is chosen – the 'suitable demos' by the utopians and the 'filtering institutions' by the realists.

Rousseau had said that only gods could have a democracy, if the solution to the dilemma of democracy is an educated and disinterested electorate. Madison, concurring, had chosen the option of the institutional filter. Constant's contribution is not in wishing to have both – that can be treated as a rhetorical flourish to round off his essay – but in drawing attention to the danger to modern liberty in unqualified democracy. Both de Tocqueville and Mill concurred.

6

SOLUTIONS
PROPOSED PART II

De Tocqueville, Mill

Alexis de Tocqueville began his classic *Democracy in America* with the claim that the phenomenon of political and social 'equality of condition' was increasing everywhere in the world, and had reached a stage in America which made that relatively new state an object lesson in how the growing impulse to equality might be managed and directed to the good. For the seemingly deterministic force of change towards equality in the nations of Europe and America

is so strong that it cannot be stopped, but it is not yet so rapid that it cannot be guided: their fate is in their hands; yet a little while and it may be so no longer. The first duty which is at this time imposed upon those who direct our affairs is to educate the democracy; to warm its faith, if that be possible; to purify its morals; to direct its energies; to substitute a knowledge of business for its inexperience, and an acquaintance with its true interests for its blind propensities; to adapt its government to time

94

and place, and to modify it in compliance with the occurrences and the actors of the age. A new science of politics is indispensable to a new world.[1]

In France, when democracy suddenly took power in the revolution, 'everything was then submitted to its caprices; it was worshipped as an idol of strength; until, when it was enfeebled by its own excesses, the legislator conceived the rash project of annihilating its power instead of instructing it and correcting it; no attempt was made to fit it to govern, but all were bent on excluding it from government'.[2]

The programme de Tocqueville is setting out in these words would seem to be one in which paternalistic institutions guide the nascent spirit of equality into a maturity and capacity resembling those of Rousseau's democratic gods, so that democracy will not be capricious and blind. Democracy is inevitable, he is saying; so let us make people fit for it. And because America has advanced further than any other country along the path of being successful at it, not least because of the nature of the people and the place, let us learn lessons from it.

On his travels in America de Tocqueville was struck by the combination of individualism and community spirit everywhere apparent. Citizens willingly involved themselves in the affairs of their neighbourhoods and neighbours, but at the same time valued and practised self-reliance. He was somewhat troubled by the conformism of American society, the danger of a 'tyranny of the majority' and of the mediocrity that could result. A mild and relaxed bourgeois satisfaction with undramatic things could be an invisible form of despotism, he said, which 'does not break wills, but softens them'.[3]

His admiration for the qualities that had made the transition to greater equality in America easy – not least among them the long tradition, stemming from the first settlers, of communal feeling – did not, however, blind him to problems, especially slavery and the treatment of Native Americans. At one point he describes seeing a group of Choctaw Indians being shipped away from their tribal homeland on a steamboat bound for Indian Territory, their abandoned dogs howling for them on the riverbank and then flinging themselves into the water to swim after them.[4]

One of the principal underlying themes of the book is de Tocqueville's anxiety about the dangers of democracy, which, because he took it to be inevitable, required to be understood and managed. One such danger lies in the spirit of equality itself: there is 'in the human heart a depraved taste for equality, which compels the weak to wish to bring the strong down to their level, and which makes men prefer equality in servitude to inequality in freedom.'[5] Likewise a refusal to defer to anyone as superior resulted in failing to make best use of those with great talents or intelligence. The gifted therefore made no greater contribution to public affairs than ordinary men, a lost opportunity. Thus does too much equality tend to mediocrity; 'it is a constant fact in the United States that the most outstanding men are rarely called to public office, and we are forced to recognize that this has occurred as democracy has gone beyond all its former limits.'[6] Moreover men of distinguished talents are often reluctant to put themselves forward in the hurly-burly of public election for the post of, say, judge; and therefore it often happens that some of the most important positions in society are not filled by the best people.

De Tocqueville's solution to the problems of democracy is conveyed in his description of two contrasts. One contrast is that between New England and the new states of the South-West. In New England, he says, one finds that education, liberty and more settled traditions have made the citizens 'used to respecting and submitting to intellectual and moral superiorities without displeasure; consequently, you see democracy in New England make better choices than anywhere else'.[7] In the South-West 'where the social body, formed yesterday, still presents only an agglomeration of adventurers or speculators, you are astounded to see what hands hold the public power, and you wonder by what force independent of legislation and men the State can grow and society prosper there'.[8]

The other contrast is between the House of Representatives and the Senate. In the former are 'village lawyers, tradesmen, or even men belonging to the lowest classes'. In the latter are 'eloquent lawyers, distinguished generals, skilled magistrates, or known statesmen'.[9] What explains the difference is that the members of the House of Representatives are directly elected, the members of the Senate are nominated by the legislatures of the states. It is, says de Tocqueville,

> sufficient for the popular will to pass through [the state legislature] in order, in a sense, to be transformed and to emerge clothed in more noble and more beautiful forms. So the men elected in this way always represent exactly the governing majority of the nation; but they represent only the elevated thoughts that circulate in its midst, the generous instincts that animate it, and not the small passions that often trouble it and the vices that dishonour it.[10]

Although often praised for his prescience, de Tocqueville is not prescient here: 'It is easy to see a moment in the future when the American republics will be forced to multiply the use of two stages in their electoral system, under pain of getting miserably lost among the pitfalls of democracy'.[11]

In short, de Tocqueville's recommendation is for a solution to the deficits of democracy framed in terms of filtering institutions, conveying the suffrage of the people by indirect means to government insulated from the 'pitfalls' and 'small passions' and 'vices' that unqualified democracy is at risk of falling prey to.

If there is a thinker who, in the period when debate about how to resolve the dilemma of democracy was at its most urgent height, was in the best position both from the historical and the theoretical point of view to formulate such a solution, it is John Stuart Mill. I do not mean by this that he devised the best solution; there are aspects of what he proposed that ring very false and would be quite unacceptable today, and indeed received much criticism in his own time. But he had before him all the theory so far reported, and the actuality of two major experiments in instituting democracy: the United States, which had devised a constitution from scratch, and the first tentative reform of representation in the United Kingdom in 1832. He wrote as further parliamentary reform was under discussion, which is why in his *Representative Government* of 1861 he devoted attention to the practicalities of franchise and voting as well as to theory, not least in relation to the arithmetic of a system of proportional representation designed to guard against the danger that he and almost every other thinker about democracy identified, viz. that of the tyranny of the majority. In his essay *On Liberty*, that tyranny was conceived to be one as much of oppressive social opinion as oppressive political dominion, and he defended freedom and experiments in living so that the best possibilities for human flourishing might be discovered. The need to protect minorities against majorities mattered to him greatly in both respects.[12]

To appreciate Mill's treatment of the topic it is instructive to look at the Reform Act of 1832 in the United Kingdom. In the second half of the eighteenth century the disabilities of those who would not subscribe to the articles of the Church of England had obliged them to found their own academies and associations, and to press for reform. Charles James Fox spoke in favour of extending the franchise during the American War of Independence, which itself helped to generate a head of steam in favour of change. The French Revolution put a stop to these endeavours, however, by prompting the British government into taking measures of active repression, including suspension of *habeas corpus* and the prosecution of leading members of the 'corresponding societies' campaigning for reform.

But by the 1820s reform was back on the agenda. Debate over emancipation of Roman Catholics had raised the question of the public's consent to major constitutional changes. The Duke of Wellington and Sir Robert Peel headed a party and an administration opposed to Catholic emancipation, supported by the king, George IV, who was vehemently hostile to it. But the election as MP of Daniel O'Connell in Ireland in 1828 and again in 1829, who as a Catholic could not take his seat in Westminster, and the long groundswell of public opinion in favour of 'Catholic relief' which had been mounting over the previous decade, obliged Wellington and Peel to change tack. They saw that public opinion was greatly in favour of emancipation, and although the election of 1826 had not turned on the matter explicitly, they were not prepared to hold out for a lost cause.

The anomaly of a Parliament in which there were MPs representing 'rotten boroughs' in some cases with no voters in them, such as Old Sarum, while large new industrial cities such as Manchester had no representation at all, glaringly made the point that in matters of important constitutional consequence Parliament could not claim that it had public support for what it proposed to do or refused to do, and now it was obvious that opinion among a far larger section of the populace than currently possessed the franchise was, as in the case of Catholic emancipation, too strongly in favour to ignore. Change was inevitable, but to begin with Wellington and Peel thought they could resist.

Feelings in the country ran high in 1830, partly as a result of the revolution in France in July of that year, which at last ousted the Bourbons from the French throne and placed a 'citizen king' on it instead. Successors of the previous century's corresponding societies, the Political Unions, served as a focus of agitation, and the election of that year was attended with strikes and uprisings. When the King's Speech for the new parliament failed to mention reform of the franchise there was uproar, and Wellington's ministry fell. He was replaced by Lord Grey, a proponent of reform. On 1 March 1831 Grey tabled a Reform Bill. A tumultuous period followed – riots, buildings set alight, strikes – until the Bill passed into law in 1832.

The significance of the Reform Act did not so much lie in the extension of the franchise – it admitted fewer than a million new voters to the roll – than in its recognition of several new principles. The chief was that the authority of the enfranchised portion of the people was required for policies that a party pledged it would carry out in government. Hitherto election outcomes had been taken as general statements of approval or otherwise for a ministry appointed by the monarch, the ministry not having pledged itself to any particular programme or policy. The Reform Act changed this. Now the endorsement of the voters was required for policies to which a party wishing to form an administration publicly committed itself in advance. Another new principle was that there should be a degree of representationality in the franchise, marked by redistributing seats from rotten boroughs to those newly large centres of population until then unrepresented.

Few of those involved in the passing of the Reform Act were aware of these consequences in full. Indeed there was a general feeling that the question of the franchise had been settled once and for all. But hindsight shows that the Act was 'the most critical in the history of the development of the people's part in government', and that the process of reform had only just begun.[13]

By the time Mill wrote *Representative Government* this fact was evident. Reflecting on the principles and practicalities involved in imminent further reform, he says: 'There is no difficulty in showing that the ideally best form of government is that in which the sovereignty, or supreme controlling power in the last resort, is vested in the entire aggregate of the community',[14] and where every citizen takes some part in the actual activity of government, even if only at a local level. Such participation would bring about 'a general degree of improvement of the community', by showing how realities demand responsibility and endeavour. He was here learning from his friend de Tocqueville who had written that Americans learned how to be democratic by participating in their local community affairs. But the ideally best form is not attainable, Mill continued, otherwise than in a very small setting, such as the ancient Greek *polis*. Therefore government has to rest on a different foundation. 'Since all cannot, in a community exceeding a single small town, participate personally in any but some very minor portions of the public business, it follows that the ideal type of a perfect government must be representative.'[15]

By 'representative government' Mill means 'that the whole people, or some numerous portion of them, exercise through deputies periodically elected by themselves the ultimate controlling power, which . . . they must possess in all its completeness'.[16] By this definition the British government is, said Mill, a representative one, and although it is in part formed by unelected bodies (the Crown, the Lords) the powers of these latter 'can only be considered as precautions which the ruling power is willing should be taken against its own errors. Such precautions have existed in all well-constructed democracies. The Athenian Constitution had many such provisions; and so has that of the United States.'[17]

Echoing the Jeffersonian idea of 'consent' Mill says that the people must be willing to accept the legitimacy of the government and its powers over them, which means also being willing to keep it standing, and to do what it asks of them. People who are unwilling to do these things, whether 'from indolence, or carelessness, or cowardice, or want of public spirit', are 'more or less unfit for liberty'.[18]

There are two chief dangers in every form of government, representative government included. The first is 'general ignorance and incapacity, or, to speak more moderately, insufficient mental qualifications, in the controlling body', the second is 'the danger of its being under the influence of interests not identical with the general welfare of the community'.[19]

The first danger is recognized as being more likely in governments that are popularly elected, given that they will tend to reflect the same level of information and cognitive capacity as the electors. The second danger, that of possible 'sinister interests' of those in power, consists in 'class legislation; of government intended for . . . the immediate benefit of the dominant class, to the lasting detriment of the whole'.[20] So it is an important question how a representative government can guard against the worst effects of these evils.

Mill's solution is a system of proportional representation that will ensure that all interests have a voice in Parliament. The technical details of the transferable votes system he suggested are irrelevant for present purpose; the principle he urged is the key thing. This is that, however Parliament's seats are selected, the result should be that 'every minority in the whole nation, consisting of a sufficiently large number to be, on principles of equal justice, entitled to be represented',[21] is indeed represented.

Once proper representation is secured, the next problem has to be addressed; namely, that 'the natural tendency of representative government, as of modern civilization, is towards collective mediocrity: and this tendency is increased by all reductions and extensions of the franchise, their effect being to place the principal power in the hands of classes more and more below the highest level of instruction in the community'.[22] Here Mill is confronting the Platonic anxiety. The tension lies between the right a citizen has to vote on national and local affairs, and the need for that vote to be used wisely. It would be 'a personal injustice to withhold from any one, unless for the prevention of greater evils, the ordinary privilege of having his voice reckoned in the disposal of affairs in which he has the same interest as other people. If he is compelled to pay, if he may be compelled to fight, if he is required implicitly to obey, he should be legally entitled to be told what for; to have his consent asked, and his opinion counted.'[23] But his opinion must, Mill adds, be 'counted at its worth, though not at more than its worth . . . though everyone ought to have a voice, that everyone should have an equal voice is a totally different proposition.'[24] Here is the tension out in the open, and Mill's tone changes. 'I regard it as wholly inadmissible,' he says,

> that any person should participate in the suffrage without being able to read, write, and, I will add, perform the common operations of arithmetic . . . It is also important, that the assembly

which votes the taxes, either general or local, should be elected exclusively by those who pay something towards the taxes imposed. Those who pay no taxes, disposing by their votes of other people's money, have every motive to be lavish and none to economize. I regard it as required by first principles, that the receipt of parish relief should be a peremptory disqualification for the franchise.[25]

In the mid-nineteenth century perhaps only half the adult population was literate (Mill was writing in 1860, and it was not until 1870 that an act was passed providing for universal elementary education). An even smaller percentage paid tax. So Mill's restriction of the franchise is quite severe. But in fact his proposals go even further. He says that, though we must accept the necessity of extending the franchise, we must at the same time counter the fact that 'in this state of things, the great majority of voters, in most countries, and emphatically in this, would be manual labourers; and the twofold danger, that of too low a standard of political intelligence, and that of class legislation, would still exist in a very perilous degree'.[26] It would be unacceptable to deny the vote on property or wealth grounds, he says, so 'the only thing which can justify reckoning one person's opinion as equivalent to more than one is individual mental superiority; and what is wanted is some approximate means of ascertaining that.'[27] Accordingly he suggests plural voting; people in occupations requiring intelligence and success should be given more than one vote.

Until there shall have been devised, and until opinion is willing to accept, some mode of plural voting which may assign to education, as such, the degree of superior influence due to it, and sufficient as a counterpoise to the numerical weight of the least educated class; for so long the benefits of completely universal suffrage cannot be obtained without bringing with them, as it appears to me, a chance of more than equivalent evils.[28]

Mill's position in these respects, like his view, when defending utilitarianism, that there is greater pleasure in reading Aeschylus than in drinking beer, is unarguably elitist, and he received so much criticism from his contemporaries as a result that he later moderated them. To counterbalance the impression these views give of him – for he was in so many respects a thinker on the side of liberty and progress – one must remember his robust championing of extending the franchise to women.[29]

As an attempt to find a way, as had Madison and almost all other theorists, to mitigate the effects of widening the franchise to those they thought would be less capable of exercising it wisely, Mill's suggestions are a failure. But the principle they sought to embed, that of *representation*, re-applied itself as having promise for a resolution to the democratic dilemma, as his arguments show; for this time it is not a 'representation' in a merely symbolic sense, but a representation intended to reflect choices at the ballot box on the part of those with the privilege of the franchise. This was in part a lucky outcome of the sheer numerousness of the represented, not all of whom could fit into a literal *agora*. Mill said that he thought the railways and the newspapers between them constituted a virtual *agora*, taking news and opinion – and indeed politicians themselves; a relatively new phenomenon – to the people who could therefore question and debate as the Athenians had. That was a largely utopian hope; but Mill sincerely wished that matters should be so.

A final point of relevance is Mill's argument that 'constitutional morality' requires that representatives should not be mere delegates, but should think and act independently in line with what they really think best. He thought this especially important

> if provision is not made for the representation of minorities, nor any difference admitted in the numerical value of votes, according to some criterion of the amount of education possessed by the voters; in that case no words can exaggerate the importance in principle of leaving an unfettered discretion to the representative; for it would then be the only chance, under universal suffrage, for any other opinions than those of the majority to be heard in Parliament.[30]

The idea of constitutional morality was borrowed by Mill from his friend George Grote, who in his great *History of Greece* had described with approval the Athenian institution of the *nomothetai*, who when occasion demanded scrutinized the laws and the practices of Athenian government for their constitutional integrity and consistency. The concept of constitutionality is naturally associated with regimes based on written constitutions, as in the United States, against which legislation and executive action can be tested. In an unwritten constitution the surrogate notion of 'constitutional morality' attempts to perform this task – a very important task, as Mill's examples show; but alas and obviously, it is too much of a convenience to an executive in a state like the United Kingdom to have the flexibility to make things up, constitutionally speaking, as it goes along, and the argument of constitutional immorality has too little purchase. A salient case in point is discussed in Appendix I.

PART II

7

ALTERNATIVE DEMOCRACIES
AND ANTI-DEMOCRACIES

We see from Part I that in the period between the mid-seventeenth century and the mid-nineteenth century – between the Putney Debates in the English Civil War and the publication of John Stuart Mill's *Representative Government* – a series of explorations was undertaken into the question of how 'the people', in some more rather than less inclusive and appropriate sense of this phrase, could be given a meaningful role in constituting or legitimizing the government of the country they live in, without the deficits that Plato and others thought would arise from this.

I have throughout described as 'the dilemma of democracy' the tension between the two desires of achieving democracy while ensuring sound and stable government, given a realistic view of what *unqualified* democracy can be. And as we have seen, the debate in the period between Putney and Mill was fundamentally and crucially focused on finding a resolution to this dilemma. In the United States a form of this resolution was instituted in practice within decades of the American Revolution. In the period between the mid-nineteenth and mid-twentieth centuries elsewhere in what came to be called 'the Western world', the resolution was implemented in a number of largely similar variants, though spectacularly and disastrously in 1930s Germany it not only failed but dragged the world into chaos. Even so, 'the democracies' won the war that this setback triggered, and survived; and since the mid-twentieth century, either in fact or by lip service, democracy has become the professed system of politics and government in the majority of the world's countries.

The resolution to the dilemma of democracy offered by thinkers from Putney to Mill is *republican* or *representative* democracy. I equate the adjectives here because the principles underlying the resolution under either heading are the same: they are that the people (strictly: the enfranchised section of the populace) are the ultimate source of political and governmental legitimacy because a majority of their votes will endorse a legislature and executive, and by the same token can dismiss them, in terms of a structure in which the expression of this endorsement or withdrawal of endorsement is periodic (in the US, for example, every four years), and follows recognized and agreed upon processes. To this location of ultimate legitimization in the endorsement of the enfranchised (the standard example is by an electoral process) is added institutions and structures which constrain the endorsed while in office. Abstracting from the ideas articulated by Montesquieu to get at the principles they in their turn embody, the fundamental idea is that decision-making and execution of decisions should be reviewable and if necessary reversible, with the reviews being undertaken by bodies separate from the legislature and executive (for example, the judiciary).

Recall that Montesquieu thought that he had derived his idea about these checks and balances from the English constitution, and his idea was acted upon by the Americans in devising their constitution; so we see the whimsical and misleading parallels between Crown and President, House of Commons and House of Representatives, House of Lords and Senate, Law Lords and Supreme Court. The disanalogy lies in the fact that increasingly the executive with its subservient majority in the House of Commons is the *de facto* sovereign body in the UK with no checks and balances on it whatever, while in the US the structure of checks and balances only works when there is consensus and is otherwise a recipe for paralysis. It would seem that as the House of Commons is the only directly elected body in the British arrangements, the fact that it is so and is all-powerful greatly bolsters its democratic credentials; but of course it is precisely the point of the representatives in the House of Commons that they are *representatives* and not delegates – that is, that they have plenipotentiary powers in their own right to decide what shall be done, independently of the wishes of those who voted for them; and that this is how things should be, given the need to improve upon, modify or correct the unconsidered and uninformed desires of voters, and often to do what is best even contrary to those desires.

It was just remarked that in the UK the executive is the *de facto* sovereign and operates with 'no checks and balances on it whatever'. Someone might object, pointing out that the House of Lords has a revising and delaying function, that the monarch can refuse to sign proposed legislation into law, and that the Supreme Court (once called the House of Lords in its guise as a sitting of the Law Lords) can request the executive to revisit legislation incompatible with the Human Rights Act. A moment's thought shows that these do not constitute vetoes, and the executive can always get its way in the end. If the Lords insist on amendments to legislation, the executive can invoke the Parliament Act which overrides them. No monarch these days – and this has been so for a long time now – would dream of refusing to give the Royal Assent to legislation; the monarchy is wholly the decorative part of the constitution and provides a useful cosmetic terminus for the legislative process only. Whereas the White House can veto bills from Congress and initiate legislation, the Crown has no power over government in either direction.

The necessity perceived by Montesquieu, Madison and Mill for a filter between the enfranchised and the government – aimed not at tricking the enfranchised out of the meaning of the imprimatur that their votes place on government, but at supplementing the process so that sound government can emerge – itself requires to be endorsed. The significance of the idea of the *consent* of the enfranchised – indeed: of the people, because the agreement of the whole people, not just those with the vote, to accept and abide by the workings of the system designed to give them government, has to be supposed – becomes apparent in this connection. The point can be made by analogy. The population of the US is vastly greater than the size of its combined police forces. A general consent to being policed is therefore a necessary condition of there being policing. The fact that the Senate in the US is not proportionally representative of the population is accepted because the right of the states to an equal say in the government of the Union is recognized. The fact that the President of the US might be elected on a minority of the popular vote is accepted because the Electoral College system – originally devised to stop unsuitable individuals reaching the Oval Office: as we see, a dead letter function now – has become traditional and American preparedness to revisit constitutional arrangements is limited in the way in which religious fundamentalism is limited in its approach to revising its views of sacred scripture.

The point of this is that the US Senate, Presidency and Supreme Court are accepted parts of a democratic system though none of the three are directly elected. They are democratic institutions, because they are thus accepted. In the UK there are persistent calls for abolition of the House of Lords on the grounds that it is unelected. It is certainly the case that the residuum of the hereditary peerage has no place in Parliament, and at time of writing this remains. But the arguments against substituting an elected second chamber for a weak revising appointed second chamber are rather strong. Who wants yet more career politicians acting in as subservient a way to the executive as in the House of Commons? People of expertise and experience might be unwilling to stand for election, doing which is about as enticing a prospect as spending a month in the village stocks as a target for rotten tomatoes. If a revising upper chamber were recognized for its utility in the process of ensuring sound government and had the consent of the people for this function, that consent being secured indirectly through the overall endorsement of the system and its legislature and executive in elections, there can be no more objection to it than there is to the US Supreme Court or the method of choosing senators and a President in that country.

Thus, in the foregoing, the idea of *representative* democracy as the resolution offered by the thinkers from Putney to Mill to the dilemma of democracy.

Has it worked? The answer is far from an unqualified Yes, and arguably it is an only slightly qualified No. A Babel of criticism and suggested alternatives has grown as the decades since the mid-twentieth century have passed, from both left and right of the political spectrum, and even from its centre. Hans-Hermann Hoppe, author of *Democracy – The God That Failed: The*

Economics and Politics of Monarchy, Democracy and Natural Order (2001), praises the libertarian criticism and proffered alternative in *Beyond Democracy* by Frank Karsten and Karel Beckman (2012). Christopher Achen and Larry Bartels in *Democracy for Realists* (2016) argue that the franchise should belong to identity groups and political parties, not individual voters, who in any case vote not as individuals but in line with their identity and party-political loyalties. Jason Brennan's *Against Democracy* (2016), pessimistic about there ever being the kind of voter essentially required by democracy, prompted a debate with Philip Pettit, the latter defending a liberal view of the democratic order as conceived by the thinkers canvassed above. Their debate in effect reprises the nub of the debate from Putney to Mill.

Prompted by the same scepticisms, David Van Reybrouck's *Against Elections: The Case for Democracy* (2015), Paul Cartledge's closing remarks in *Democracy: A Life* (2016), theorists of 'deliberative democracy' inspired by Jürgen Habermas and John Rawls, proponents of anarchy, proponents of various forms of direct democracy such as the Occupy Movement's advocacy and use of 'participatory democracy', government by referenda, government by sortition (lottery) – all these suggestions and alternatives reflect a dissatisfaction with the systems that call themselves democratic.

One of the phenomena singled out for special attention because it appears to capture the dissatisfaction that the peoples in democracies feel towards democracy as it has emerged in recent history, is populism. It is prompted by the feeling that government is too remote and too unresponsive to concerns at the grass-roots level, and accordingly takes the form of an upswelling of indignation and a desire to get attention and remedy. Populism leads variously to revolution at one end of the spectrum, to surprise outcomes in elections at the other. The years between 2010 and 2016, from North Africa and the Middle East to Western Europe and North America – that is, from the 'Arab Spring' to the Brexit and Trump phenomena in the UK and US respectively – would appear to constitute an exhibition of perfect examples of the entire spectrum of what populism is and can do. But it is arguable that in at least some of the Arab Spring movements, for example in Egypt and Syria, the first steps in revolution were not populist but led by vanguards of intellectuals seeking civil liberties and some form of democracy. Revolutions are not often inherited by those who start them, as history feelingly teaches, and Egypt, to take just one example, starkly demonstrates this. But populism seems certainly to be in play in other cases; the surprise results at the ballot box in the UK and US in 2016 are attributed to it by many experienced commentators.

A telling characterization of populism is offered by political philosopher Raphaël Liogier:

> Populism should not be confused with demagoguery, which is a natural tendency in representative democracies, a temptation to seduce voters rather than convince them. Nor is populism about being in touch with the people. Rather, it is the claim to speak in the people's place, in their name, and convey an undeniable shared truth on their behalf. In particular, populism claims to express the emotion of a people that feels beleaguered, diminished and lost. Its discourse is nostalgic for past power and wedded to a frantic defence of identity.[1]

On some views, the reappearance of populism in Europe after the Cold War is a result of the end of that stand-off, which had provided everyone with a focus for fears and anxieties, with an 'other' in the form of communism and the Soviet bloc as threats to blame for discontents – or for governments to persuade their populaces to bear with discontents. In not much more than a decade from the fall of the Berlin Wall in 1989, a new Other had emerged in the form of Muslim immigrants, hostility towards whom was inflamed by acts of terrorism by activists claiming to act on behalf of the Islamic faith. Populist political parties rose on the anti-immigrant tide: Geert Wilders' Party for Freedom in the Netherlands, the Danish People's Party of Pia Kjaersgaard, the inaptly named Party of the Democratic Centre in Switzerland, Sweden's National Democrats, the National Front in France led by Marine Le Pen, the Jobbik Party in Hungary, the Austrian Freedom Party – note the characteristic invocation of 'freedom' and 'democracy' by xenophobic (too often just racist) and nationalist parties of the right – all both harness and inflame anti-immigrant sentiment. Such parties flourish on demagoguery, gaining support by exploiting the worries and antipathies of people only some of whom would be likely to enjoy much freedom or democracy if the parties in question gained power.

The sentiment that gives rise to populism, namely that government serves only the elite that constitutes it and is too remote and uncaring about problems at the grassroots, when allied to the feeling that immigration is responsible for unemployment, stagnant living standards, and poor functioning of health, education and welfare services, gives rise to predictable outcomes. Inequality in standards of living is a great destabilizer of society – not poverty as such, but the differential between high earners and those on middle and low incomes. When inequality grows, when the gap between the top and bottom in society becomes palpably great, trouble ensues. This is an emphatic lesson of history. Demagogues able to blame inequality on immigration or on the uncaring self-serving elites controlling government, or both, can thereby promote a populist upswelling, from which they themselves profit. They can then seek to remould the political and economic order to their own preferred pattern, which of course is not often likely to be an improvement for the people whose support they have exploited to do so.

As is often the case, the problem is one of differences between perception and reality. In the complexities of numerous and diverse societies, where competing interests, expensive demands, the relative impotence of government in many areas of social life, and the political process itself, there will always be individuals and groups dissatisfied with their lot and with what government is doing or failing to do about it. The problem can be summed up by looking at it from the perspective of politics rather than from that of the populace, and observing that it is a rare political career that does not end in failure, however much celebration attended its beginning: Tony Blair's prime ministership affords a paradigm case. Government has accordingly and aptly been likened to 'herding cats'. In part, and one suspects in large part, lack of understanding of the nature and limitations of government, and of the workings of the political process, contribute to populist resentment, some of which therefore is unjustified. The remedy is education, a point of wider significance to which I return below. Where it is justified, however – and it often enough is – the remedy lies in the responsibility both of politicians and government to address their own failure to explain, justify and include; and not least, to their own damaging propensity to promise too much in order to get elected in the first place.

There are those who extol populism as an authentic expression of democracy. They see it as real democracy, true democracy. They see it as it is in its moment: and the image they have of it is that of the demonstration, the march, the crowd at one with itself, its members united, determined and optimistic. Whoever has been on a march or demonstration will recognize the feeling of solidarity, and the joyful sense that people power is true power. In that moment the best of what unified action and solidarity can be is manifest. Are, however, such events always correctly identified as *populist*? The crowds in Tahrir Square in Cairo at the beginning of the Egyptian revolution against President Mubarak were not populist crowds. Were the events in Leipzig in the German Democratic Republic before the Berlin Wall came down in 1989, in Prague's Wenceslas Square at the same time, examples of populist triumph? Consider the students in Beijing's Tiananmen Square in June of that same year, in the activism which itself prompted the events in Eastern Europe later in the year; does that constitute an example of populism? One would say not: a sociology of politics might disentangle the taxonomies of democratic attitudes and actions, of which populism is assuredly a species, but it would not be surprising to find that the ticklish question of social demographics enters the distinction. The kind of reasons Mill had for espousing plural voting reappear, here as every time the ochlocratic spectre arises in connection with direct democracy, popular feeling, the rise of xenophobia and nationalism generally.

Hannah Arendt distinguished between the 'masses' and 'the people' in her *Origins of Totalitarianism* (1951). The latter wish to see their views and wishes make a difference; the former hate the society which they feel has marginalized and excluded them. Unless a leader emerges to direct their anger and put it to work for longer than the space of a riot, the masses are mere collocations of individuals. In the second (1958) edition of her book she observes that the feelings of superfluousness and isolation which are characteristic of individual members of the mass makes them ripe for harvesting by demagogues for totalitarian causes. They can be of any or all classes; the mass is not a class phenomenon. The key is political alienation and the disengagement from the society's political and economic life, until circumstances make the individuals in question throw themselves into the mind of the crowd in their anger or despair.

It is easy enough to see why populism rouses the opposition of those for whom a resolution to the dilemma of democracy matters. Populist sentiment is the element in which demagogues swim. Demogogues thrive on simple slogans, where serious politics requires examination of detail. Minority rights are important for democracy; the demagogue cares only for the enthusiasms, prejudices and demands of the majority. Eloquence instead of attention span, the immediate instead of the long term, the local and obvious instead of the larger picture and all the depths and dimensions it contains: these things are the preoccupations of the populist crowd and therefore the demagogue exploits them to sway its mood. Populism exists as a political emotion, it expresses itself in the form of attitudes rather than worked-out ideas. It is therefore antithetical to the kind of democracy that the resolvers of the democratic dilemma sought for the sake of sound government, because it forgets that the participation of the enfranchised is, though a necessary condition, not a sufficient condition for that soundness.

There is a connection between populism and the rise of the use of the term 'democracy' which for many, and especially the conservative elements in society, was still a term of malediction even into the early twentieth century. In his famous address at Gettysburg, Abraham Lincoln invoked the Declaration of Independence rather than the Constitution in saying that the test which the Civil War was imposing on America was whether 'government of the people, by the people, for the people, shall not perish from the earth'. He was criticized by Union anti-abolitionists because in this speech and in the emancipation proclamation he was ignoring the Constitution's acceptance of slavery and its lack of reference to equality, and he was doing it by a populist appeal to 'the people' rather than to the institutions so elaborately put in place for government of the people. Such is the power of prepositions: 'by' is a far cry from 'for', and one can make what one likes of the ambiguity of 'of'.

By the middle of the First World War, and especially when Woodrow Wilson led the United States into it, it had become convenient to invoke democracy as the value that the war was being fought to protect. This made the word 'democracy' fully respectable at last. As often happens, the propagandist expedient of promoting democracy to a great value of civilization proved as much of a convenience as a burden subsequently; totalitarian regimes fell over themselves to describe themselves as 'People's Democratic Republics' and one justification offered for the 2003 Iraq War was that it was taking democracy to the suffering people of that country.

It is, though, worth noticing in passing that not all populisms of the twentieth century annexed the word 'democracy'. 'National Socialism' succeeded in harvesting populist sentiment while eschewing it. Once the National Socialists – the Nazis – had harvested the sentiment, they quickly ensured that democracy would be firmly and securely quashed.

There is much to admire and applaud in the optimistic endeavours of those who propose both 'deliberative democracy' and 'participatory democracy', for their ambitions are premised on a positive attitude to the *demos* as being apt for either. These are views that are natural for someone on the political left to wish to believe in, because they valorize the people and place the source of political power and legitimacy squarely where such an orientation says it should be: in their hands.

Deliberative democracy is the democracy of debate, discussion, the mutual giving of reasons with the aim of reaching agreement or consensus upon which decisions can then be based. It distinguishes itself from 'aggregative democracy' where the sum, or the majority, of preferences as expressed in a vote determines what is to be done, and it concentrates instead on the discursive process in which views can be transformed and brought into fruitful mutual convergence by discussion.

'Participatory democracy' began, at least as a phrase, in the student movements of the American 1960s, but achieved the status of a theory in Carole Pateman's *Participation and Democratic Theory* (1970). She sees 'participation' as meaning 'equal participation in the making of decisions', and 'equality' as referring to 'equality of power in determining the outcome of decisions'. The locus of participation is the citizen body; it makes the decisions, and their decisions are carried out by officials. It is a form of direct democracy, and is consistent with deliberative democracy because of course the desideratum is good decisions for the appointed officials to implement. 'The justification for a democratic system in the participatory theory of democracy', says Pateman, 'rests primarily on the human results that accrue from the participatory process.'[2]

The question to be asked about these alternatives for democracy, which critics argue are frankly utopian, is whether there is reason to believe that the members of the *demos* who will deliberate, give each other the reasons they owe each other in the process of transforming views to achieve convergence, or participate together in decision-making, have moved on so far from the anxieties Plato had about them, that the second half of the democratic dilemma has ceased to be applicable. If they have – if the people possess the information, the commitment to and capacity for rational evaluation, and the other requisites for producing sound government which the scepticism of Plato denied them – then these forms of democracy are ideal.

Pateman stated her theory in express opposition to the view which had classic status when she wrote, namely Joseph Schumpeter's suggestion about a system of democracy which he thought improved on the 'classical view' that emerged from the Putney to Mill debate. In his *Capitalism, Socialism and Democracy* (1943) he argued that democracy is not about arriving at particular ideologically defined outcomes, but instead, and quite differently, is a method for arriving at decisions. He thought the 'classical view' of democracy was wrong because of the assumption that there is a 'common good' and a correlative 'common will' which aims at attaining the common good. Accordingly he defined classical democracy as 'that institutional arrangement for arriving at political decisions which realizes the common good by making the people itself decide issues through the election of individuals who are to assemble to carry out their will'.[3] In what is in effect a reprise of the Platonic argument he cites the observations of Gustave Le Bon and later social scientists on the psychology of crowds, which he says reveal

> the realities of human behavior when under the influence of agglomeration – in particular the sudden disappearance, in a state of excitement, of moral restraints and civilized modes of thinking and feeling, the sudden eruption of primitive impulses, infantilisms and criminal propensities – [Le Bon] made us face gruesome facts that everybody knew but nobody wished to see and he thereby dealt a serious blow to the picture of man's nature which underlies the classical doctrine of democracy . . .

the phenomena of crowd psychology are by no means confined to mobs rioting in the narrow streets of a Latin town. Every parliament, every committee, every council of war composed of a dozen generals in their sixties, displays, in however mild a form, some of those features that stand out so glaringly in the case of the rabble, in particular a reduced sense of responsibility, a lower level of energy of thought and greater sensitiveness to non-logical influences. Moreover, those phenomena are not confined to a crowd in the sense of a physical agglomeration of many people. Newspaper readers, radio audiences, members of a party even if not physically gathered together are terribly easy to work up into a psychological crowd and into a state of frenzy in which attempt at rational argument only spurs the animal spirits.[4]

Schumpeter argued that we should see democracy instead as a competition for the popular suffrage between individuals or parties seeking the power to make decisions in government. 'The democratic method is that institutional arrangement for arriving at political decisions in which individuals acquire the power to decide by means of a competitive struggle for the people's vote.'[5] If to 'individual' is added 'or party', this comes close to the reality of electoral democracy in at least many of the countries describing themselves as democratic today.

If Schumpeter was unconvinced that the crowd at an election hustings in 1940s America was notably different from that in the Athenian *agora* as Plato knew it, one could fast-forward to the present and ask whether grounds for believing in the possibility of deliberative or participatory democracy have since improved. In the view of Jason Brennan they have not.

There is an instructive debate between Brennan and Philip Pettit on this head, not least because the latter defends a version of the dilemma resolution that emerged from the Putney to Mill debate which is, however, not a version of what Schumpeter questionably called the 'classical model'. That model turns on the correlative ideas of a common good and a common will which aims at it. A more realistic idea is of a pluralistic society in which compromises, and sometimes uncomfortable accommodations between unresolvably competing interests, have to be managed in a process which is itself always under negotiation, not least in the form of periodic elections and changes of government. It is a mainly unstated assumption of the dilemma resolution model of representative government that this is how things are; and this I take to be implicit in Pettit's view.

Brennan argues that people have a right to good government, but democracy as at present constituted does not give it to them, because electorates are irrational and insufficiently informed, and their self-interest and short-termism results in their making poor choices from the point of view of what would most benefit the state, the economy, the entire community. Mill and others had argued, taking their cue from what de Tocqueville thought he saw in America, that political engagement does people good and educates them; Brennan argues that not only is this not true but the opposite holds, for what happens instead is that democratic participation makes people meaner and more entrenched in their biases and irrationality. Therefore, he argues, we should try the experiment of replacing democracy by epistocracy – rule by the knowledgeable.

This is pure Plato, both as to diagnosis of the problem and the suggested alternative; and it constitutes a rejection of the idea that the institutions and practices of a democratic order could so filter the ochlocratic tendencies of a *demos* as to produce sound government while also having its consent. Brennan's reason for this last point is the failure of the democracies with these institutions and practices: they are evidently not working, he says, and the ignorance and irrationality of electorates are in the driving seat. He would doubtless cite Trump and Brexit as stark proof of this claim.

The debate with Pettit goes straight to the crux of the problem for Brennan.[6] While agreeing that democracy has been the least bad of a lot of bad systems so far, he thinks we can do better, not least because democracy disincentivizes people from acting wisely. 'Since individual votes count for so little, each voter can afford to be ignorant and misinformed about politics, or to indulge her worst biases and delusions. Imagine if a professor in a 1000-person class told her students she would average their final exam grades together and they'd each get the same grade. They wouldn't bother to study, and the average grade would be an F. So it goes with voters.'[7] The problem is endemic: 'Voters usually do not know the basic facts relevant to the election. They also have silly and mistaken beliefs about the social sciences and suffer from a wide range of cognitive biases that prevent them from thinking clearly about politics. As numerous studies have shown, if voters were better informed, they would have different political preferences. They vote the way they vote, and we get the candidates we get, because voters are ignorant, irrational, and misinformed.'[8]

Is not the independence of representatives a specific against this problem, just as representative democracy requires? Brennan acknowledges that this is true, but it still happens often enough that governments respond to voter preferences and accordingly introduce into the system the deficits they contribute. In fact, he argues, democracy does not empower individuals, it empowers collectives of which individuals are part – thereby actually disempowering the individuals in them.

If there were a system of government that produced demonstrably better outcomes for society than democracy does, he asks, would it not be perverse not to adopt it? After all, systems of government are merely tools for the achievement of ends; it is rational to adopt the best tools therefore. Getting the good government to which everyone has a right does not necessarily require, and indeed might be better without, the 'universal equal adult suffrage' that supporters of democracy so fetishize.

Pettit's answer is a classic statement of the republican or representative view. 'If democracy is equivalent to electoral rule, considered independently of other institutions, then it is surely overrated. If it is equated with a richer package that includes elections as one amongst a set of complementary institutional elements, then it is not.'[9] Russia and Turkey provide examples of polities where leaders are elected, but where there are no institutions or practices to constrain their behaviour in office. Such institutions and practices include 'various checks and balances, the separation of powers, rights of speech, assembly, and open contestation, courts of appeals, limits on campaign finance and lobbying, and the like'.[10] These empower the citizenry to contest the activities of their representatives, they 'will do this by putting obstacles or costs or difficulties in the way of any authorities who try to abuse their power',[11] and thus reduce the domination that governments might exercise over individuals.

But the crucial difference between Pettit's view and Brennan's lies in the former's emphatic espousal of the principle of universal equal adult suffrage, even though he acknowledges that the latter's observations about 'voter ignorance and irrationality are broadly correct'.[12] His reason is that universal suffrage best embodies what democracy is for, namely to promote observance of such standards as that no one is of less than equal status, that different does not mean unequal, and that equality independently of gender, ethnicity and sexual orientation is the ideal. And he takes it that universal suffrage helps to force those in government to adhere broadly to such standards. 'Democracy on this understanding operates to good effect over the long haul, where that effect may not be obvious in the hurly burly of short-term, electoral politics.'[13]

Why is universal suffrage indispensable to securing these desiderata? A sceptic about democracy might ask why a benign dictatorship could not achieve this, doubtless more quickly and with less difficulty. If someone responds that the trouble with dictatorships, benign or otherwise, is that what happens in them can change on the whim of the dictator, the sceptic can reply that the whim of the electorate can be no less fickle. Brennan's response to Pettit's argument comes down in essence to asking why universal suffrage is especially the best way to attain the ideals associated with democracy.

I think the answer lies in the justifications one can give for the source of legitimacy in politics and government. The question any putative leader or government has to answer is: 'By what right do you presume to make laws and direct our society? Who has given you the authority, the power, so to do this?' The various answers of the past – this sword in my strong right arm, my charisma, my wealth, my wisdom, the support of my fellow nobles, God – might have echoes today in (say) 'the army' and in some quarters still 'God'; but none of these answers, at least in the 'West', hold much water. The answer 'because the major-ity of us agree', has come to be where justification stops: it is where the spade is turned as one digs a foundation on which to stand political authority. Moreover it is persuasive, for it satisfies associated commitments to ideas about the right we have, as citizens, to be consulted and involved, to have our views take effect, to be able to free ourselves from government we dislike.

The fact that these rights and the engagement they permit clash with the generally recognized lack of aptitude to make best use of them is not a reason to deny the rights, but to build a structure in which their exercise can be fruitful – the structure of republican or representative democracy.

Opposition to representative democracy from those who extol deliberative, participatory or direct democracy tends to come, as noted, from the left of the political spectrum, dissatisfied with the operation of the democratic systems that have evolved from the Putney to Mill debate. The political right has a different take altogether. Their opposition is to democracy in any of its forms. The motivations for libertarian and anarchist views are, though expressed in a variety of ways, strongly possessed of Wittgenstein's 'family resemblance' feature.

The chief prompt for the political right's attitude to democracy is the question of liberty. The possibility of an uneasy relationship between liberty and democracy, certainly the threat to minorities represented by majoritarianism, are concerns that found a resonance in all the architects of representative democracy, not least Benjamin Constant for whom it was a crucial matter; and addressing those concerns is precisely the purpose of the institutions and practices required to ensure sound government and the protection of civil liberties. The protections cut two ways; minorities are protected by regimes of rights from oppression by majorities, and everyone is protected from excessive interference or oppression by governments.

But libertarian anxiety about threats to liberty go further than institutional assurances can easily assuage. Democratic government by its nature responds to many of the demands of the majority for such things as welfare spending, public health and education provision, environmental protection, subsidized transport, and more. This makes for big government. The minority that thinks it provides the economy's driving force – entrepreneurship, job creation, generation of much of the national wealth – want smaller government and lower taxes than would meet democratic demands. The argument is not just about management and size of the public economy. The freedom of the individual is limited by having to walk in step with others, indeed by any measures that promote equality given that liberty is a naturally inequality-fostering value. Democracy is accordingly seen by libertarians as a threat in ways that subvert not merely civil liberties but self-determination and self-creation at a profounder level – the existential level.

Libertarians recognize that proponents of 'small government' will find it hard to be elected into positions of power by democratic majorities, because they see that their argument that most areas of social and economic life should be off limits to public policy initiatives will not sit well with those actively promoting the latter in the interests of equality and justice. Libertarians believe that societies spontaneously generate ways of living with themselves, analogously with market forces finding the right price point for a commodity or service. And they regard this as desirable, because government can only deal with problems in the mass, at the lowest common denominator, whereas the organic activities of an unregulated society promote fine-tuned activity addressed to the specific and the particular.

The objection to libertarian views is obvious. In the absence of constraints, the strong dominate the weak – think of Thucydides' report of what the Athenians said to the besieged citizens of Melos in the Peloponnesian War, warning them that they would be massacred if they did not submit: 'let us not waste time talking of right and wrong', they said, 'for the strong do what they will, and the weak accept what they must'.[14]

Government, such as it is, will be captured by money, big business, vested interests – in short, by whoever the strong are. Society will be run on terms set by whichever interest group is most powerful. Some version of the Hobbesian state of nature is recreated by the absence of structures and agreements constitutive of civil society and its values; there does not have to be a literal jungle for its laws to apply.

Representative democracy has attracted so much criticism from across the political spectrum because it is perceived to have functioned ill, and to have failed too many in the societies in which it is the political regime. It does not matter that by almost all measures the citizens of democracies (the Western democracies at least) are safer, wealthier and freer than human beings have ever been anywhere in history and across the non-democracies today. Social dissatisfactions are relative things, and income inequality and unfair distribution of opportunities rankle. The foregoing touches on some of the complaints made about representative democracy; some of the complaints are justified; it is time to look at what has gone wrong with the solution to democracy's dilemma proposed by the tradition of thought between Putney and Mill.

8

WHY IT HAS GONE WRONG

There are three main reasons why representative democracy has failed to deliver on the promise of its design. One relates to the operation of the institutions and practices of the dilemma-resolving model itself. The second relates to those in whose hands lies the ultimate source of legitimation of the democratic political order – the electorate. The third relates to manipulation of both the two former by agencies with partisan interests which would not have much chance of succeeding if in open competition with other political orientations on the hustings.

The first is failure of the systems constituting representative democracy to operate as the theory of them prescribed, mainly because those who take control of them, to begin with through the normal democratic process, deliberately redirect them in ways more convenient for the practice of government or, less benignly, for their own class or party-political interests.

The second is the failure to equip the *demos* for their part in the process; this is particularly so regarding the civic education required to make representative democracy work. More to the point: the problem here is the absence of such civic education. Both horns of the dilemma of democracy relate to the *demos* – the desire that it should be the giver of the imprimatur for government, and the problem of its actual or alleged unfitness to do so. Most of those who have thought about the matter simply accept Plato's assumption that the *demos* will ever be unfit; de Tocqueville and Mill more optimistically spoke of the good that would come of greater popular engagement and responsibility; the former thought he saw it already happening in America, the latter thought that it needed work, and until then those among the people already fitted to be the *demos* of a democracy should have an extra vote accordingly.

The third is interference and manipulation by agencies with partisan interests who recognize that they are unlikely to get their interests favoured in mainstream ways otherwise, and who therefore resort to undemocratic means to get the democracy to deliver their preferred outcomes.

The second point mainly speaks for itself, given that in the debate about how to resolve the dilemma of democracy it has precisely been the self-defeating potential of the *demos* in its uninformed, uncritical, self-interested myopia that is identified as a danger to sound government. I return to consider it in another context later, and here I will mention it in connection with the third point. I therefore focus on the first and third points, taking them in turn.

The best illustration of the first reason for the relative failure of representative democracy is Parliament and parliamentary government in the United Kingdom.

In the United Kingdom the doctrine of the sovereignty of Parliament, as it developed after the settlement of 1688, is exactly what it says it is: an explicit claim that no other body, neither the Crown nor the people, is sovereign. This remains the constitutional position today. Savour the full force of this doctrine: it is Parliament which is sovereign, not 'the people'. What Wellington and Peel said about the relationship of Parliament to the wishes of the people (that the job of MPs is to 'deliberate upon matters of common concern, and to decide according to the best of their judgement' and not merely be messengers mechanically carrying out the wishes of an electorate) therefore technically remains true. But there has been a further development. The powers of part of Parliament, namely the House of Commons, have increased with every extension of the franchise to embrace all adults (with specified exceptions and on the shifting basis of views about the age at which adulthood begins), while the powers of the Crown and the House of Lords – the other two parts of Parliament – have respectively become nugatory and all but nugatory over the same period. So the sovereign body in the United Kingdom is not Parliament as such, but only part of it: the House of Commons.

But even this is no longer correct, and has not been correct for quite some time. For the *de facto* sovereign is not the House of Commons but the executive commanding a majority in the House of Commons. This is because of the system of party discipline exerted by the Whips, the party police who ensure that the executive receives the votes of the members of the party from which it is drawn in the House of Commons. So the true situation in the United Kingdom is that the ministry, the administration, with its subservient voting bloc in the House of Commons where a single vote majority can enact or suspend any law whatever, any civil liberty or human right whatever, has absolute power.

It is important to note what this means in practice. The executive – in the UK called 'the ministry' – is technically appointed by the Crown, and increasingly since 1688 exercises the Crown's powers, though the occasional constitutional quarrel arises over whether the 'Crown prerogative' – the Crown's powers to make treaties and, by 'Orders in Council', laws without parliamentary involvement – remain in the ministry's hands, so that it can act on its own authority as the Crown once did without Parliament. The device of Orders in Council is rarely used, but the prerogative power remains in respect of treaties; though when treaties confer rights on British citizens, as the European Union treaties do, Parliament has to be consulted – this was confirmed in a 2016 Supreme Court decision on the matter, when the UK government tried to bypass parliamentary discussion about whether to trigger Article 50 of the Lisbon Treaty to take the UK out of the EU, but in a judicial review was told by the Supreme Court that the matter required parliamentary approval.

Recall that a recurrent theme in thinking about how democracy is to be translated into sound and stable government requires balances provided by the institutions of democracy and its practices. In the United Kingdom institutional checks on the power of the executive have reduced dramatically, not increased; the absolute authority of the executive through its subservient majority in the House of Commons has grown greatly as the influence of the second chamber and the head of state has waned into almost nothing, and the inability of the courts to check the executive has been restricted to judicial review and advising on incompatibility with the Human Rights Act – which of course government on the political right in the UK wishes therefore to repeal.

In a Dimbleby Lecture for the BBC in October 1976 Lord Hailsham QC, a former Lord Chancellor and Cabinet minister, described the British system of government as an 'elective dictatorship' and called for a written constitution. The central defect in the British system, he said, consists in

> the absolute powers we confer on our sovereign body, and the concentration of those powers in an executive government formed out of one party which does not always fairly represent the popular will. I have come to think that . . . [the solution is] nothing less than a written constitution of the United Kingdom, and by that I mean one which limits the powers of Parliament and provides a means of enforcing these limitations both by political and by legal means.[1]

Most who understand the principles underlying the concept of representative democracy would see Hailsham's diagnosis as correct, and his proposed solution as right. The fact of *de facto* dictatorship is of course the worst of it; but other problems are created by the situation too. As the independence of members of the House of Commons has decreased under the system of party discipline – it is known as 'whipping' by analogy with the fox hunting practice of whipping packs of hounds into order for the pursuit – so both the quality and reputation of MPs has declined, rendering them even less likely to behave independently. The lack of independence of MPs adds to the low estimation in which politicians are held by the general public, as does their lack of genuine influence, as individual MPs, in dealing with problems faced by constituents. The questions both of quality and degree of influence are important, because if MPs had the ability in both relevant senses to make a genuine difference to local and national issues alike, the respect in which they are held, and the ambition of able people to offer themselves for the role, would increase.

The question of whipping is almost never discussed, but it is arguably a serious matter of constitutional import. It can be reasonably argued that MPs can be whipped by their party managers to support legislation promised in an election manifesto on the basis of which they were elected. In all other matters it is unacceptable that MPs should be required to vote in line with the executive's wishes whatever their own individual judgment. It is common knowledge that the party Whips press MPs to toe the line with promises and threats. Rebels are warned that they will not be offered ministerial posts, or will not receive support for re-election; so much is admitted by any MP you ask. If MPs hold either an actual or a 'shadow' ministerial post, or serve as a Parliamentary Private Secretary to one such, they are expected to resign if they defy the whip. If a backbencher repeatedly refuses to obey the whip, suspension can follow, with loss of privileges, access to party meetings, and support. Defying the whip is regarded as a very serious matter.

This is bad enough: it is illegal in every other workplace in the country to secure compliance with bosses' wishes by threats analogous to these. This is harassment and coercion. How can this be acceptable in Parliament? It is *permitted* because the precincts of Parliament are *outside the law of the land*, and within the boundaries of the Palace of Westminster MPs can do many things with literal impunity for which they would be arrested outside. Some of these privileges are important for free speech: no one can be libelled in Parliament, for example. But MPs do not avail themselves of this particular privilege in the way that most matters often enough or in the most crucial circumstances – holding the executive to account, challenging it, refusing it the *carte blanche* that the whipping system gives it – and yet these particular undesirable privileges are regularly exercised by the party Whips.

All this, to repeat, is bad enough. But matters are even worse. Not only are threats used, but bribes – and how can it be either legally or morally acceptable that MPs can be made to vote as the executive wishes by suborning them with the offer of advancement or support? And not just bribes, but blackmail – stories circulate of Whips telling recalcitrant MPs that their private affairs and peccadilloes will be leaked, damaging their personal lives and reputations as well as their careers. In our society revelations of marital infidelity, or of the fact of being homosexual without wishing to avow that one is, are nobody's business, but the tabloid press makes a field day of such matters, and a politician's life and career can be seriously jeopardized as a result.

The 'three Bs' of the Whips, 'bribery, blackmail and bullying' as MPs themselves call it – each of them in quite literal sense; there is said to be a case where an MP was forced into the desired lobby with his arm twisted up behind his back – might be permitted by the arcane provisions of parliamentary privilege, but they are not acceptable, illegal anywhere but in the Palace of Westminster, and fundamentally subversive of democratic principles and the duty of MPs to constituents and the country.

The practice of whipping parliamentary votes is therefore a serious anomaly not just because in every other workplace it would be illegal, but because it distorts and undermines the representative process. An egregious example is the passing of the vote in the House of Commons in February 2017 on the triggering of Article 50 for taking the United Kingdom out of the European Union. The majority of MPs on all sides of the House were 'Remainers' in the EU referendum of the previous year. But they were whipped into supporting the bill providing for the triggering of Article 50. Even as they traipsed into the lobby to do so, many of them stated that they knew it was wrong, disastrous for the country, against their considered opinion, and not what they wished. Yet they voted against their knowledge and judgment because ordered to do so, and whipped to do so. In all conscience, how can such a situation be allowed to prevail? In allowing that whipping might be justified for legislation promised in an election manifesto, one is implying that if legislation is actually contrary to an election promise, there would be even greater turpitude in whipping the vote for it. Yet this indeed was the case with the Article 50 vote: the government had been elected in 2015 on a promise to keep the United Kingdom in the European single market, and to campaign for continued membership of the European Union.

To these distortions of the original purpose of representative democracy must be added the problem of the electoral system. Many of the abuses of an elective dictatorship using coercive means to ensure that it effects its programme would be prevented by a system of proportional representation and the consequent likelihood of coalition government. Proportional representation is a simple matter of fairness and appropriateness; the moderating effect of coalition in government is a simple matter of desirability. Opponents of proportional representation dislike it precisely because it prevents one party getting its way without hindrance when in government; 'strong government' is the phrase employed as if such a thing were invariably a good.

It is easy to show what is so badly wrong with the first-past-the-post (FPTP) system in use in parliamentary elections in the UK and for the House of Representatives in the US.

In such a system whoever gets 'the most' votes in each constituency wins that constituency. Suppose in a given constituency there are one hundred voters and ten candidates. Suppose eight candidates get ten votes each, one gets nine votes, and one gets eleven votes. The person with eleven votes 'wins'; he got 'the most votes' in the sense that he got more than anyone else did. Or, more accurately: he got more votes than any one other person individually did. Result: eighty-nine out of the hundred voters in that constituency have no representation in Parliament; only eleven do. That is the system in UK-wide general elections. It is very rare that an MP gets more than 50% of the votes cast in a constituency, but even if he or she did, why should the other 49% or 30% of votes – or whatever the proportion – mean nothing? If out of a hundred voters sixty vote for A and forty for B, in the resulting make-up of Parliament there should be a 60–40 distribution of representation, or close to it. That is simple fairness and appropriateness. The usual effect of the first-past-the-post system is that British governments are minority governments, standardly based on about 35% of the vote (and therefore an even smaller percentage of the total electorate). On this kind of percentage, given the distorting effects of electoral geography, a party can have an unassailable majority in the House of Commons, and therefore in principle – because there is no constraining constitution specifying the limit of what the majority can do – dictatorial power.

Is there a tension between the idea of representation proportional to votes cast by the enfranchised part of the populace, on the one hand, and on the other hand the idea that representation is something that can be exercised independently of a direct bestowal of suffrage, as with the consent that the *indirectly* elected parts of the US political order enjoys? Recall that the phrase 'unqualified democracy' in earlier pages here denotes circumstances in which a people, or the enfranchised part of it, have their directly expressed will directly acted upon by the executive which serves them. There are two ways in which, by contrast, a democracy might be qualified, dependent on the two senses of the word 'qualified' that are relevant. One is where the nature of the enfranchised is such that sound and stable government flows from their will because they are informed, reflective, well-judging, altruistic, and long-termist in their views. The other is where the institutions which the enfranchised part of the people consent to be governed by are such that, given that their will can often be the opposite of the qualities just listed, a filter is in place which enables more considered and rational action to be taken in the interests of the whole state and not just a perhaps impassioned sectional interest in it.

The ideas of Madison, Mill and the other thinkers discussed embody efforts to ensure sound government by means of the latter form of qualification – that is, by having workable institutional arrangements and practices in place in the political order that parlay and when necessary modify voter preferences into sound government. They concur with each other in thinking that the franchise and the enfranchised's choices in elections are only part of what would make for a functioning democracy. If one thinks it utopian to hope for an informed, reflective, unprejudiced, disinterested, dispassionate, altruistic, and well-judging populace which thinks of the interests of others and the long term, one is bound to recognize the force of their view.

The question is whether such arrangements work. Did they work in the United States as Madison hoped they would? The answer is rather dispiriting: for in the United States the deliberately indirect forms of representation for three of the four chief institutions of state, their powers intended to be mutually counterbalancing, have not succeeded in overcoming factionalism. Rather, the violence of the opposition between Republicans and Democrats is such that the entire country is frequently paralysed by their mutual hostility.

The remark that representatives have the duty to 'deliberate upon matters of common concern, and to decide according to the best of their judgment', and not merely be messengers mechanically carrying out the wishes of an electorate; the commendation of acting on 'the reason and calm judgment of this House [rather than on] the feelings and wishes of the people'; the idea that the government, though not all its organs are wholly constituted by popular franchise, can be 'the faithful representative of the sense of the country'; all these things might have been said by Madison or Jefferson as they constructed the constitutional system of their new country. In fact the first was said by the Duke of Wellington in opposing parliamentary reform in 1832, the second by Sir Robert Peel in agreeing with him, and the third is a comment made by Charles James Fox at the time of the American Revolution, indicting those opposed to parliamentary reform on the ground that they thought they represented 'the sense of the country' without needing the votes of its inhabitants to prove it.

On such views it might seem that FPTP is just another device to filter out the full force of popular desires. But to think this is to mistake the point of the filter in the paradigm of representative democracy. The institutions and practices in question are intended to be agreed, transparent, not manipulable by individuals or parties, and such as to bring more careful examination and review of policy, expressing the thought that it is better to do well than quickly. One important part of the structure is the endorsement given by the enfranchised to the system, while at the same time expressing preferences on matters of policy. In the FPTP voting system all but those who vote for the 'winner' – in our example, just eleven of the hundred voted for the 'winner' – are effectively disenfranchised; the votes of the eighty-nine give them no voice; there is no difference between their voting and their not voting so far as that is concerned. One of a number of problems this causes is that individuals think it is not worth voting, especially in constituencies which have traditionally returned candidates from the same political party. But the malevolent operation of this system is that *not* to vote actually *supports* whoever receives more votes than any one other candidate, by enhancing his or her chances of doing so!

These considerations illustrate how a political order which is meant to be an instance of representative democracy fails by a wide margin to be one, operating in such a way as to be far from embodying the solution that the theorists of representative democracy intended.

The next point is interference and manipulation by agencies who recognize that they are unlikely to get their interests favoured in mainstream ways, and who therefore resort to undemocratic means to achieve their political aims.

A wholly proper feature of democratic politics is the effort made by those seeking the votes of the enfranchised to put a programme before them and to persuade them of its value. It is also legitimate for them to criticize the proposals of their opponents, and for third parties – newspapers, special interest groups – to comment, criticize, support or endorse what politicians are saying. The hustings now include television addresses, debates and advertisements.

This picture of a vigorous democratic debate summoning the enfranchised to make a choice is of course idealized. In practice the process involves spin and dirty tricks, half-truths and untruths, distortion, propaganda, *ad hominem* attacks on individuals rather than their ideas, all aimed at inflating the positives of one party and undermining the credibility of the other. Matters have always been so. In ancient Athens the sophists promised to teach the skill of arguing either side of the same case with equal plausibility and success, with an eye to the law courts and the politics of the *agora*. Propaganda has always been a tool of politics and by its nature does not pretend to be a

channel of truth and accuracy. There have always been demagogues playing on the hopes and fears, the prejudices and
desires, the anger or the nationalist sentiment, of a populace. In
recent history Benito Mussolini and Adolf Hitler stand out as
paradigmatic demagogues. Less obvious candidates for demagoguery are the owners of newspapers which push the owner's
agenda, sometimes in undisguisedly propagandistic ways; think
of the *Sun, Daily Mail* and *Daily Express* as egregious examples
of this in the UK.

All these phenomena put pressure on the reliability of the
democratic process. In recent times they have been supple-
mented, perhaps supplanted, by other more powerful and, if the
full extent of fears about them are borne out, too often more
sinister forms of manipulation of opinion and sentiment. Already
well understood is the use of Big Data as a highly contemporary
way of achieving demagogic effects. Other forms of hidden
persuasion, and of interference with electoral processes, are
made possible by computer hacking techniques. There were
claims of interference of this kind in the US presidential election
of 2016, allegedly perpetrated by Russian agencies, and similarly
in the Brexit referendum in the UK in the same year and in various European elections in 2017. Fake news was certainly a more
than usually salient feature of political events in this period, and
was linked to the interference. It is easy to get carried away by
conspiracy theories, including those that go on to indict the
so-called 'deep state' in various countries for influencing and
sometimes interfering with the governments there; but in these
cases there might well be grounds for concern.

A report by two *New York Times* journalists reads as follows:

In a development that can only heighten the distrust between
American and Russian authorities on cybersecurity, the Justice

Department on Wednesday charged two Russian intelligence officers with directing a sweeping criminal conspiracy that broke into 500 million Yahoo accounts in 2014 ...

Details of the wide-ranging attack come as the United States government is investigating other Russian cyberattacks against American targets, including the theft of emails last year from the Democratic National Committee and attempts to break in to state election systems. Investigators are also examining communications between associates of President Trump and Russian officials that occurred during the presidential campaign ...

On Wednesday, prosecutors unsealed an indictment containing 47 criminal charges against the two agents of Russia's Federal Security Service, or FSB, as well as two outside hackers ... [2]

On the same day, the BBC announced a collaboration with a journalism project called 'CrossCheck', set up by First Draft News, 'to verify and debunk fake stories surrounding the upcoming French elections'. The first false story they exposed was that presidential candidate Emmanuel Macron was receiving campaign finance from Saudi Arabia. Concerns in France about fundamentalist Islamic terrorism, given the horrifying Charlie Hebdo, Bataclan and other attacks, would make any such link inflammatory, given Saudi support for the Wahhabi form of Islam often associated with extremism.

In June 2017 a *Guardian* newspaper report entitled 'Pay to Sway' revealed how easy and relatively inexpensive it is to manipulate elections by these means. 'Political campaigns can manipulate elections by spending as little as $400,000 on fake news and propaganda,' it said, adding that the cost of instigating street protests is $200,000, while discrediting a journalist costs

$55,000. The report continued, 'Chinese, Russian, Middle Eastern, and English-based fake news services found that these options offer a cost-effective alternative to traditional advertising and promotional efforts, often by manipulating social networks to spread dubious content.'[3]

Reports such as these more likely than not touch on tips of icebergs. A related area of serious concern is the use of Big Data techniques in election campaigning, a development not only troubling in itself as applied to opinion formation in elections – in medical research and elsewhere in science Big Data is a boon – but it suggests the technical power that is undoubtedly in play in these other cases.

Big Data works by trawling huge amounts of data on social media and then analysing it using powerful AI technology. By this means fine-grained psychometric profiles of individual voters can be produced. By identifying voters' emotional triggers it shows campaign teams what messages and advertisements can be tailored to those emotions. Rules on what is admissible in electioneering, most particularly in relation to the amounts of money that can be spent in the course of an election campaign, have not been updated to take account of this, an important matter because much of the development of these techniques, and the profiling on which the actual electioneering takes place, will have incurred its costs well before the electioneering period begins, which means that the expenditure involved does not have to be declared. The *Observer* newspaper reported that 'a leading expert on the impact of technology on elections', Martin Moore of King's College London, regards this development as 'extremely disturbing and quite sinister' because 'undisclosed support-in-kind ... undermines the whole basis of our electoral system, [which is] that we should have a level playing field.' Details of how people were being targeted with this technology raised even more serious questions, he said; "We have no idea what people are being shown or not, which makes it frankly sinister.'[4]

This point about transparency is an important one. We are all now the subjects of profiling and the targets of tailor-made messaging as a result; Google not only profiles us on the basis of our internet searches so that it can choose which advertisements to place on the screens of our laptops, but it also decides what we might like to know when we are in search of information – note this: it does not direct us to information, generically considered, but to information suited to our individual profile. This is troubling enough. But in the case of political messaging such targeting is even less acceptable. Political messaging by its nature is invariably partisan, tendentious, and even propagandistic; and if it is being fine-tuned to pull our individual 'emotional triggers' it amounts to manipulation, and manipulation of which we are unaware. That is subversion of what should be an open and transparent process. If I found that I had been subjected to such targeting on the basis of profiling, it would be of great relevance to know which individuals or organisations were behind it because then I could properly evaluate the messages I was receiving.

In an essay entitled 'Confronting a Nightmare for Democracy' media experts Justin Hendrix and David Carroll report their concerns about 'hypertargeting':

In the aftermath of the 2016 Brexit referendum and US presidential election, much has been written about how personal data was used to target voters with advertisements and other messages over social media. We've since learned that actors both foreign and domestic employed information operations, computational propaganda, and cyberattacks weaponizing our commercial media infrastructure. The question at hand is whether our democratic process can endure a hyper-personalized data-driven media and propaganda environment . . . What we fear is a future in which potent personal data is combined with increasingly sophisticated technology to produce and deliver unaccountable personalized media and messages at a national scale . . . Deploying hypertargeted voter media that constructs narrow or outright fabricated versions of the truth to influence small subsets of voters in strategically important geographies is a scenario our founding fathers never imagined.[5]

Hidden persuaders have their easiest time with ingenuous persuadees. It was not an original discovery on the part of Daniel Kahneman that people divide into what he calls 'fast' and 'slow' thinkers. Bertrand Russell famously said, 'Most people would rather die than think, and most people do', and an anecdote about Adlai Stevenson in the 1952 US presidential election sums up the matter perfectly; told by an ardent supporter that he would definitely receive the votes of every thinking person in the United States, Stevenson replied: 'I'm glad to hear it; but I need a majority.' Campaign managers have long known that the more manipulable of the populace constitute that majority, and have acted accordingly. Joseph Goebbels encapsulated the basic method: say something often enough and loud enough and people will believe it. Big Data and computer hacking techniques merely add a great access of range, speed and power to this old and tried process. But the use of the familiar techniques for propagandizing the multitudes, in the safe knowledge that they will not scrutinize what they are being told but will quite likely just believe it, would seem to have become more brazen of late. Claims known to be false and promises known to be unfulfillable have their desired effect on first being issued, and the effect is not nullified by subsequent modification or withdrawal.

A senior BBC news editor told this writer that during the EU referendum campaign of 2016 in the UK, the BBC were aware that they were reporting statements and press releases which, when they had tracked down and challenged those who had issued them, would be modified or withdrawn, and that therefore they were simply serving the interests of a campaign propaganda machine – but helplessly so, given that they had a responsibility to report the day's news.

Notice what is happening. Plato feared the collapse of democracy into ochlocracy – that the uninformed, prejudiced, self-interested, emotionally driven many would take power, and bad government would follow. History shows the extreme example of this, in the form of revolutionary mobs introducing arbitrary rule, and soon enough anarchy and chaos, into which tyranny steps to take control. But in our present day highly sophisticated techniques are employed by partisan interests to target different facets of the uninformed, prejudiced, self-interested, emotionally driven attitudes of different constituencies of the many, to aggregate them into voting for an outcome which is the partisan interest's own preference. In the Trump and Brexit outcomes, the partisan interests involved are not concerned with the desires of at least most of those they corralled into voting for them; in both the Trump and Brexit cases, the interests are of a minority seeking the freedom for themselves to profit.[7] The aim of the architects of representative democracy was to prevent a single interest from dominating: in the distortions that representative democracy has suffered, new manipulators have found a way to pervert that aim.

Conspiracy theorists are probably not completely wrong in thinking that there is another potential enemy of democracy in the 'deep state', the network of civilian and military officials who influence, sometimes control, and even sometimes undermine democratically elected governments. One can imagine that they might sometimes protect democracy too, against leaders who, perhaps put in place by a populist upsurge, begin to dismantle what in normal times provides protections of civil liberties and human rights.

The person who has done most in the period immediately before the writing of these pages to make the concepts of the deep state and of fake news prominent, is none other than Donald Trump, President of the United States. He blames the deep state for thwarting his policy initiatives – there were many in the first days of his occupancy of the White House, in the form of a snowstorm of executive orders – and fake news for falsifying his support in the country, minimizing the crowds at his inauguration, and more.

There is a consensus among observers of world affairs that a number of countries, Pakistan and Egypt often cited among them, are greatly influenced by shadowy bureaucracies of military and government officials. One imagines that in those places the power of the deep state is rather direct, not least as a result of the politicization of the security and intelligence services and the judiciary. In the US and the UK the use of leaks, rumour, go-slow obstruction of policies unwelcome to the bureaucracy, are doubtless commonplace; whether anything more fundamental happens is an interesting speculation. But even the modest activities described do not have a place in a democratic order, and must be thought questionable.

Outright thwarting of government policies which began life as manifesto commitments would obviously be unacceptable, but that does not mean officials should not have views, proffer advice, and summon precedents from experience. If 'deep state' only denotes the permanent officials and career security personnel who serve the state, there is no objection to it. However, the sinister idea of it working to undermine democratically elected governments and democratically approved policies is where the problem lies. The culture of the state officials service, and the institutions which govern its activity, together ought to be able to insure against sinister possibilities.

Talk of a 'deep state' reminds one of the talk of 'dark money' – undeclared financing of campaigns, bribes to officials or elected representatives, undeclared party donations or donations whose full extent is not made public. 'Dark money' is just the easiest currency of something that might better be called 'dark influence', which can be exercised without cash changing hands, but instead by a weekend on a yacht in the Mediterranean, facilitation of a contract, the exchange of sensitive information of any kind, introduction to an obliging companion at a house party. Dark influence can be rewarded with titles and honours in the UK, with lucrative contracts and access to the corridors of power there and in the US and indeed everywhere. All this too is subversive of democracy, though it is older and more commonplace by far than any form of democracy.

A study by academics at the London School of Economics (LSE) in early 2017 confirmed that spending on the Leave campaign in the European Union referendum of June 2016 was 'almost entirely unregulated or even recorded'.[8] Most of the cost of the campaign was incurred before the period in which spending is monitored, not least in the building of the databases used for Big Data targeting of messages to prospective voters. Add the fact that there is no transparency about who is sending the messages and for what ulterior purposes other than aggregating the votes of different groups identified as persuadable, and anxieties about corrupt practices grow.

One of the LSE team investigating the use of 'dark money', Professor Damian Tambini, said, 'We don't have a system that is working any more. In this country, we have had laws to control spending by political campaigns but online campaigning has changed everything and none of the existing laws covers it. The ability to throw around large amounts of cash is almost completely uncontrolled. The key costs in campaigning – building the databases – is happening during the period when campaign spending is not regulated at all.'⁹

Talk of 'dark money' of course brings to mind money as such, dark or otherwise. If there is one monumental barrier to democracy in the US it is the enormous sums of money disbursed on elections, and the effect this has of making the US dangerously close to being a plutocracy where the highest office in the land goes to the highest bidder for it. To stand for President, even as an independent, a person must have tens of millions of dollars available. Money is required for election campaigns everywhere, of course, but in many polities there are upper limits on what can be spent, and the spend has to be declared to a watchdog tasked with ensuring as level a playing field as possible for the process. In the US the limit of the electoral spend is the appetite of donors – or what they hope to get out of being donors.

Representative democracy suffers, and has suffered, because of these corrosions within it. When people feel that it is unresponsive, remote, run by elites for their own benefit, and therefore not delivering, it is partly because of these obstacles to its functioning well. It is also partly because expectations of government are too high, and partly because government is not being frank about the difficulties any complex society and economy faces. And it is also partly because those in politics and government fail in some aspect of maintaining the transparency, communication and explanation that the task of leadership imposes. Taken together, these considerations go a long way to explaining disenchantment with representative democracy. Seeing these considerations thus set out also, however, indicates what the remedies might be: as to which, some suggestions are made in the following chapter.

.

9

MAKING REPRESENTATIVE
GOVERNMENT WORK

My proposal on this matter is as simple as it will be contentious. It is that the solution to the dilemma of democracy proposed by the thinkers earlier discussed is right, and will work if implemented properly, vigorously, clearly, and fully.

Sensible human beings are not perfectibilists but meliorists. They do not expect perfection, but believe in trying to make things better, and in putting things right and improving them when they do not work well enough. They remember that the best can be the enemy of the good; the failings and frailties of human institutions, like those of human individuals, are inevitable; but there are many things that have to be the very best they can be – medical procedures, airline journeys, maintaining the security of bank accounts – because of what is at stake. Government falls into this category. Yet it is perennially at risk because government emerges from politics. It was somewhat utopian of James Madison to hope that faction – party divisions and differences – might be kept away from interfering with government; that is the same as hoping that politics can be kept out of politics. But the desire to structure *government* so that the whims and passions of the enfranchised can be transformed into good government might be thought to parallel a desire to achieve by those same methods a transformation of faction into good government. To some extent that it is a reasonable hope, except of course that the personnel of government include the factionalists themselves, and the deficits of government show how easily that hope can be dashed.

But the main target of the debate that allowed democracy to emerge in modern times, after its long Plato-induced proscription, was the dilemma of how to gain the will of the enfranchised to legitimize government, while ensuring that government is sound and stable and acts for all.

The words 'unqualified democracy' in the foregoing pages describes a situation in which a people, or the enfranchised part of it, have their directly expressed will directly acted upon by the executive which serves them. As already mentioned, there are two ways in which, by contrast, a democracy might be qualified. One is where the nature of the enfranchised people is such that sound and stable government flows from their will because they are informed, reflective, well-judging, altruistic, and long-termist in their views. The other is where the institutions which the enfranchised part of the people consent to be governed by are such that, given that their will can often be the opposite of the qualities just listed, a filter is in place which enables more considered and rational action to be taken in the interests of the country as a whole and not just a perhaps impassioned sectional interest in it.

The filter is the institutions and practices which make for informed deliberation and choice of policy. Those elected have to be fit for the purpose of acquiring information, examining it, listening to arguments relating to it, forming judgments, submitting their judgments to the scrutiny of others, changing their minds if they encounter evidence and reasons that compel a change of mind – and reaching decisions that responsibly address the interests of more than their own partisan loyalties. The elected therefore have to be *representatives* in the full meaning of this term, not messengers or delegates merely relaying – independently of what they come to know by being engaged full time in the business of government whether in the governing party or an opposition party – the majority wish of those who voted for them. Their responsibility as representatives was famously described by Edmund Burke:

> Certainly, gentlemen, it ought to be the happiness and glory of a representative to live in the strictest union, the closest correspondence, and the most unreserved communication with his constituents. Their wishes ought to have great weight with him; their opinion, high respect; their business, unremitted attention. It is his duty to sacrifice his repose, his pleasures, his satisfactions, to theirs; and above all, ever, and in all cases, to prefer their interest to his own. But his unbiassed opinion, his mature judgment, his enlightened conscience, he ought not to sacrifice to you, to any man, or to any set of men living. These he does not derive from your pleasure; no, nor from the law and the constitution. They are a trust from Providence, for the abuse of which he is deeply answerable. Your representative owes you, not his industry only, but his judgment; and he betrays, instead of serving you, if he sacrifices it to your opinion.[1]

Add to this the legitimate independence of representatives from the coercions of party discipline in all matters other than the policy platform they subscribed to in being elected, and the paradigm is set.

Representatives nevertheless ought to be representative in the different but allied sense of being elected by means of a system that gives a fair indication of voters' preferences, and provides voters with representatives to whom they have given a measure of endorsement. Some systems of proportional representation allow numerous small and sometimes extreme parties to hold the balance of power in coalitions – the systems of Israel and Italy are cases in point – but it is not difficult to guard against this.

A legislature ought to be different in personnel from the associated executive, and a bicameral legislature in which a more directly elected chamber can have its proposals reviewed and discussed by a less directly elected and – importantly – less powerful chamber not constituted on exactly the same party lines as the former, captures the unarguable proposal of Montesquieu for the safeguard of second thoughts and extra time to have them in. The powers, rights and duties of all three bodies should be clearly laid out in a constitution which at the same time specifies the rights and liberties of individuals and minorities in the polity, and there should be a Supreme Court empowered to strike down legislation, or acts of the executive, that are in violation of the constitution. Thoughtful and methodical ways of keeping the constitution itself responsive over time to social change should be specified in it.

In elections there should be complete transparency about funding, and about who is involved directly or indirectly in campaigning and what they are contributing to the side they support. Limits on the amount that can be spent on campaigns help to level the playing field between different parties. Media reporting and lobbying should be rigorously kept to standards of probity and accuracy, with severe penalties for infringements. Opinion polling should cease a week before voting day, and betting on outcomes should be forbidden as particularly distorting and vulnerable to manipulation.

All this seems to me the least that is meant by the idea of republican or representative institutions aimed at increasing the chances of sound government when the authority of such government is accorded it by a democratic suffrage. This is, as it were, the bottom line in plain terms of the ideas that emerged over the two centuries to Mill's *Representative Government*. If actually applied and operated it would capture what those thinkers saw as the answer to the dilemma of democracy.

On some of these points the bones require more flesh, as follows.

In the Introduction I said that there are other reasons why representative democracy should be preserved – but properly operated in line with its founding intentions in resolving the dilemma of democracy.

One is that if citizens knew that if they lived in a state with a reliably constrained and responsible government *because of the constitutional checks in place*, which they had voted into office with their informed approval of what it proposes to do, and which they could vote out again in another election fairly soon if needs be, they could get on with all the other interests and demands of their lives in the reasonable confidence that they are not going to be cheated by it in some way. The heated nature of party politics, on show in debates in the UK's House of Commons and the poisonous confrontations within the Washington DC beltway, is premised on the supposition that the other party are indeed trying to cheat everyone, so that they require constant anxious monitoring and the constant ringing of alarm bells. This has the effect simultaneously of unnerving the populace and making it disaffected with politics. If there is no difference in the hysterical pitch of the political conversation between discussion of workaday matters of government, on the one hand, and debate about great questions of principle on the other hand, people naturally become less able to distinguish between them, and less effective contributors to either.

Of course people should be informed about what is happening in government and politics. Attending to the news – if the news media themselves can be relied upon to separate reportage from opining and persuading – is a sensible grown-up thing to do. And from time to time it might be necessary to take political action as a result of what one learns. But whereas politicians think that politics is everything, all-consuming and all-important, and that it is imperative to follow the political cycle of events without drawing breath, the truth is that there are many equally and often more important things in the lives of the great majority of people, and they want to get on with them. Confidence in reliable institutions and practices of government, populated by constitutionally constrained operators of them voted in and votable out by the enfranchised, would lower the political temperature of society in the required way.

This is not to preach inattention either to politics or government, or lack of participation in either. It is to reduce the useless part of the noise surrounding both. Devotees of politics think that everything political is a matter of high philosophical principle, which is why they conduct themselves at fever pitch. Occasionally this is necessary. Arranging matters so that it is not generally necessary would do everyone much good.

I said in the Introduction that a major part of the problem with politics is politics itself, and that the place of the political in the life of a state or national community should be considerably smaller than it currently is. This is not, note, a recommendation for 'smaller government'; it is a recommendation for more mature political activity. The foregoing paragraphs explain what I mean by this. Doubtlessly, however, some will object to such a view, because it appears to run counter to an ideal of participation which Machiavelli revived in the sixteenth century from the ethos of the Roman republic, and which came to be significant for those who thought about how to make democracy work in the American Revolution of the late eighteenth century. This was the idea, sometimes called 'civic republicanism', that citizens have a duty to be active in affairs of state; that just by virtue of being a citizen one should participate in decision-making, and should seek office when appropriate. Although this ideal is not the same thing as democracy, it seems naturally to be connected with it; both involve having a say or a part in the government of one's society.

Benjamin Constant cast this ideal of participation in different terms, seeing it as an expression of a form of liberty. He described what he called the 'ancient view of liberty' as the view that to be, or to be part of, the source of political authority over oneself, one must participate in its exercise. He contrasted this with the view he attributed to the 'moderns' of his own day: 'The aim of the ancients was the sharing of social power among the citizens of the same fatherland: this is what they called liberty. The aim of the moderns is the enjoyment of liberty in private pleasures, and they call "liberty" the guarantees accorded by institutions to these pleasures.'[2] Quentin Skinner has argued forcefully for a similar distinction between 'republican liberty' and the idea of absence of constraint that Hobbes succeeded in making the dominant conception of liberty from his own time onwards. For Skinner, to live under the rule of another even if that other does not interfere with one's activities is in principle to be not genuinely free, though in practice unconstrained.[3]

Liberty and what we mean by it emphatically matters.[4] But in the present context I think there are two slippages in Constant's view, the one being the question of how liberty is attained and exercised, the other being the question of whether 'the moderns' desire liberty in order to 'enjoy private pleasures' in a sense that trivializes the private sphere; that is not Constant's intention, and nor should it be ours.

On the first point, it is not impossible to imagine situations where liberty prevails but which are not democracies: so-called 'enlightened despotism' might, if genuinely enlightened and benign, provide an example. This will not be Skinnerian republican liberty, of course, but (see the footnote above) it will be liberty in every sense intended by Hobbes, Isaiah Berlin and every standard regime of human rights and civil liberties. In fact of course constitutional democracies are the best guarantors of liberty we can conceive; relying on the goodwill of a dictator to be and to remain benign does not quite compare.

On the second point, there would be something deliberately reductive in saying that the 'moderns' desire liberty in order to 'enjoy private pleasures' where these are thought of as essentially trivial. It is more accurate to say that they desire liberty in order to get on with private life, and to pursue aims which, given the diversity of human nature and interests, might be very different from those chosen by their neighbours. As already remarked, this is not to say that one's country should be run on autopilot so that one need never think about it. Keeping abreast, acting when necessary, voting thoughtfully at election times, are certainly civic responsibilities. What one objects to is the frenetic activity of party politics day in and day out which both numbs and exhausts public interest in government, and thereby does the polity a disservice.

The other thesis mentioned in the Introduction is the need for compulsory civic education in schools, and compulsory voting for all aged sixteen and above. The reasons are as follows.

No form of democracy can protect itself either from degenerating into ochlocracy or being hijacked by a hidden oligarchy – of money, big business, the arms industry, partisan groups intent on hijacking the system for their own benefit only – unless the enfranchised are informed and reflective. The first defence against both is a thorough understanding of the institutions and practices of the democratic order and the government it licenses. This means understanding the constitution, the political process, the extent and limits of legislative and executive competence, the responsibilities and role of the enfranchised themselves, and the political opportunities of the populace as a whole.

Voting should be a civic responsibility from sixteen years of age for two powerful reasons: that what people learn at school about these matters can be applied straight away, and that if voting begins at sixteen in the context of civic education there will be a greater chance of responsible and thoughtful voting continuing thereafter.

Voting should be compulsory, as it is in Australia. It is a duty comparable to obeying the law and paying taxes. Not voting has the practical consequence of being a form of voting – and a particularly dangerous one, because it abdicates choice to the resulting minority of voters who therefore become the majority of whatever number of votes is cast. In a first-past-the-post system, as noted, non-votes always effectively support the winning side, which, precisely because of the non-voters, will almost always be a minority of the whole.

To see this – and one must keep giving these examples: the point matters so much – suppose you have a group of one hundred people who belong to a certain club, and they are asked whether as a group they should leave the club or remain in it. The question on the ballot paper is: 'Should our group leave the club, Yes or No?' Suppose thirty of them do not vote, thirty-seven of them vote Yes, and the remaining thirty-three vote No. The Yes vote wins, despite being just a little over a third of the members of the group. In effect the thirty non-voters have supported the Yes vote, even though it is quite likely that the abstention of many of them suggests that they are either content with the status quo (i.e. remaining in the club) or indifferent to it, which is to say, at the very least not so actively keen to quit the club as to go out and vote to do so. Only those among the non-voters who wish to have their minds made up by others will not be victims of their own inactivity; they will have got what they wanted in this limited, irrelevant and feeble sense.[5]

In compulsory voting people who do not like any of the candidates, or do not wish to express a view, can spoil their ballot papers, thereby registering a protest. That is a valid expression of opinion or sentiment. But not voting at all, not being bothered to give the matter some thought and to get to a polling station, is frankly to be condemned, given that the vote is something it took centuries and much bloodshed to get, and is therefore no trifling possession. Disenfranchising oneself is a sin that should be a crime.

A third point I mentioned concerned the fact that in a numerous, diverse and complex pluralistic society the task of managing competing needs and demands is an important one, and that representative democracy does it better than competing systems. I described this task of the political order as one of negotiation, in which reconciling and accommodating differences is a continuous process, rarely completed, never without residue in the form of lingering grievance on one side or lingering dissatisfaction on the other; such is the nature of a multitudinous people jostling together, and having to jostle together perforce, with much to disagree as well as agree about. In direct democracy the power relations between different interests have no separate and defined forum in which the application of other considerations – rights, constitutional requirements – might serve as a check on what an imbalance of power could effect. In a deliberative democracy entrenched differences might fracture the system altogether, if there is no separate and defined forum – a parliament or congress of representatives, structured as such – with the power and duty to intervene.

There is no consensus in any large society about all the elements of the common good. Venn diagrams of desiderata will overlap, but there will be many circles, and some will not impinge on others at all. In such a case there needs to be a mechanism for managing the Babel of claims and demands, the equally valid but not always consistent interests and needs, the legitimate but hard-to-satisfy and often inconsistent ambitions, of the groups and individuals which form the great mosaic of society. To do this with justice and sensitivity, in a framework that respects individual and minority rights, is a demanding matter. The political and governmental order needs to be as fit as possible for the purpose. Of all the systems we know – save an absolute dictatorship whose subjects are willingly subservient, perhaps – a representative democracy with institutions and practices that filter from the tumult what is needful, what is right, what is as good as can genuinely be achieved, is the answer that the great debate on democracy gives us.

10

THE PEOPLE AND THE CONSTITUTION

Throughout the foregoing I have used expressions such as 'the enfranchised', 'the *demos*', because of the often tendentious and always potentially misleading notion of 'the people'. The populace and 'the people' are not the same thing, neither in fact nor in political discourse, which makes the concept of 'the people' too easily manipulated. In political contexts 'the people' means 'those who have the vote', but the blurring between 'people' and 'populace' (or 'population'), as these terms are used in more general contexts, allows politicians to give the impression that 'a majority of those who cast a vote' means 'everyone in the whole population' by sliding illegitimately between the two senses. This is what pro-Brexit politicians constantly did following the EU referendum of 2016; there 26% of the whole population cast a vote to leave the EU, yet the pro-Brexit politicians claimed that 'the people had spoken', 'Britain has voted to leave', and the like. What adds to the difficulty is that the idea of 'the consent of the people' is the idea of something that could be variously acquired or assumed on a basis other than, as well as by, the casting of votes; here 'the people' would indeed mean everyone if they were 'represented' by (say) the aristocracy or the king.

There is a frank admission in practically all of the discussions that whoever 'the people' are – whether all the adult males, or the wealthier adult males, or all adults for a defined 'all' turning on the age at which adulthood status is accorded – a direct democracy of them would not guarantee sound and stable government, and too likely the reverse. One can try some thought experiments here. Suppose legislation is effected by referenda. Bills are published, a period of time is allowed for the populace to read them, there is debate on radio and television scheduled especially to coincide with this period and monitored for information and balance. Voting then takes place via the internet, the populace logging in with their passwords to cast their electronic ballots. In the utopias described by Montesquieu and Rousseau where the populace is virtuous, altruistic, intelligently informed, and reflective, such a system would be a near-perfect democracy. The chief objections to such a system arise from the realistic acceptance that such utopias do not exist. Objectors would confidently predict low participation, rapidly falling to a very small percentage of the population, uneven distribution of expertise, and the ever-present chance that the theorists' greatest bugbears of emotion, prejudice and ignorance will distort the process, as happens with upswells of populism.

A simpler and yet more direct system, not taxing the efforts and understanding of the populace as much as the foregoing, would be daily referenda on yes-no propositions. In the morning a proposition would appear on television screens, in homes and in shop windows for those without a television at home. With the buttons on the handset viewers enter their pin, then select Yes or No. The majority carries the day without further reflection or debate. In this scenario it is easy to imagine that favourite populist themes would be enacted: use of the death penalty, and for a wider range of crimes including paedophilia and perhaps also homosexuality, as public attitudes harden and the power of the instant ballot unleashes yet more prejudices, and more anger, fear and resentment, as happened to a surprising extent after the Brexit referendum of 2016 in the United Kingdom, and after the election of President Trump in the USA at the end of that same year.

Representative democracy should have no truck with referenda. A referendum is an opinion poll, in which the profile of sentiment in the population, as it stands on the day of the vote, is measured. It puts a question, usually complex, to be answered by a simple yes or no. The representatives in a representative democracy are charged with getting information, listening to arguments, forming a judgment, and justifying it; none of this is required of a voter in a referendum. They can and typically do cast their vote on the basis of what they feel or believe or desire, with there being no guarantee that any of these things are the outcome of informed rational deliberation and choice. Often enough their views on polling day might be the outcome of what campaigners have told them in the weeks beforehand. Yet proponents of the yes and no answers can claim outrageous things, make promises, mislead, predict, and warn, all unaccountably; there will be no come-back against them afterwards.

If, however, representatives abdicate their duty and delegate their decision-making responsibilities to a referendum, two necessities have to be observed. The first is that everyone who might be affected by the outcome of the referendum should have a vote in it, from the age of sixteen upwards; and that there should be a supermajority threshold if the referendum could result in any major change in the affairs of the nation. Such supermajorities are standardly set at two-thirds or four-fifths either of votes cast or – more correctly – of the entire electorate.[1]

The reason for rehearsing these points is that, as John Stuart Mill said in *Representative Government*, there is a 'constitutional morality' which inconsistencies and wavering applications of principle violate. It does not merely appear, it *is*, the case that governments of the day make it up as they go along with respect to what they are going to countenance, accept, understand, and do – there is no firm understanding of what a referendum requires – why the franchise for it must be the widest relevant franchise possible, why a supermajority should be standardly required, why everyone should know what actions will follow on the outcome. In the case of the EU referendum of 2016 and the subsequent interpretation of the result that the Brexit-keen government placed on it, there is a strong taint of political illegitimacy and constitutional immorality in Mill's sense.

The key notion in Jefferson's view, and arguably for representative democracy as such, is that of *consent*. Jefferson's phrase is 'the consent of the governed', which can sound patronizing and paternalistic unless the emphasis is placed where it belongs, on the word 'consent' itself. A better phrase would be 'the consent of the people', but for reasons to do with the systematically misleading nature of the phrase 'the people' it would be more accurate, and therefore yet better still, to say 'the consent of the enfranchised'.

A virtue of this latter formulation is that a significant point is kept in view: that there is no such thing as a democracy of a whole people – of everyone from birth to death, in every station of life – but instead that every franchise is restricted or qualified. The phrase 'universal adult suffrage' is equally misleading because 'adult' is defined as applying to people over a certain age who have not been disqualified by a prison sentence or (in the UK) by being a peer, and who count as citizens or as non-citizens with certain rights such as (in the UK) citizens of Eire and Commonwealth countries – and therefore again, not everyone.

The qualification of the franchise is itself a political matter; the questions, each vexed, that have to be addressed are: who has the vote, what kind of vote should they have, and should franchises for general elections and referenda be the same or should the latter be more inclusive?

Consider the second question first: what kind of vote should the enfranchised have? This is a question about the electoral system. In a first-past-the-post system as employed in UK general elections, a vote for a losing candidate is the same as no vote at all, because it secures no representation for the voter. He or she has to be content to be represented by someone on the other side of the argument from them. The system disenfranchises all losing voters. However, if voters are prepared to accept this situation, they thereby consent to be governed by those to whom the system gives governmental power. But there is a problem with this point, to which I return below.

The question of who gets the vote is the same as the question of who gets a say, however far the voter is from the actual exercise of power. There has therefore always been an implicit question of franchise in all forms of rule. In an absolute monarchy there is one vote; in an oligarchy, a few; and so forth. Formalization of enfranchisement is again implicit in arrangements specifying the relationship between rulers and subordinates, as for example between the barons and the Crown in England's Magna Carta. Giving the barons rights against the Crown is in effect to give them something like a vote in government, because at the very least it constrains the exercise of governmental power in specified respects. From the introduction of parliamentary systems (let us say, from de Montfort's parliament of 1265[2]) the reality of a distribution and sharing of power, turning at bottom on the existence of consent or veto, had explicitly arrived. The ascendancy of Parliament over Crown in the English case was at last won, with bloodshed, in the seventeenth century's Civil War and Glorious Revolution, the first effectively if indirectly preparing the ground for the second.

Parliament was always representative, from the outset; the question was who was represented, and how consent was given for that representation. Casting a vote to elect a member of Parliament is an act of explicit consent. Accepting that there is a parliament and that one must abide by the laws it passes, even if one did not have a vote and had no say in who sits in that parliament, is or is at least claimed to be implicit consent. Those who voted for the system and those who did not but who accept it and obey the laws it passes seem to be on the same footing: they both consent or fail to register dissent, which in practice amounts to the same thing from the point of view of those in power.

This way with the idea of consent, however, raises a problem. On this basis one could argue that dictators whose diktats are obeyed have, in that obedience, a demonstration of consent to their rule. But one might answer that there is no question of consent here, only of submission on prudential grounds, when dictators enforce their rule by coercive means – bullying and violence, fear, the threat of torture or of being 'disappeared'. To this in turn a riposte might be that the coercion employed to enforce compliance – let consent fall where it may – differs only in manner and degree between a modern liberal democracy and the most tyrannical of tyrannies. In the former someone who flouts the law might be fined or imprisoned; in the latter they might be flayed, buried alive, crucified or impaled. The *principle* that sanctions will be applied unless the government's rule is accepted and obeyed is the same.

What therefore is the significance of consent? The most obvious point is that there is a world of difference between being party to instituting these or those sanctions, on the rational ground that observance of laws is necessary for achievement of the ends they serve, and having them imposed on one without having been consulted about them. But in fact this is a problem even for a liberal democracy with the widest and most inclusive franchise of the standard type, for there will always be many without a vote; if voting 'adulthood' begins at sixteen then it is the fifteen year olds and younger; if the franchise is restricted to 'citizens' then migrant workers who pay taxes (they might be senior bankers and consultant heart surgeons as well as plumbers, nurses and building labourers) are excluded, in defiance of the fundamental concept of 'no taxation without representation'.

This returns us to the question of 'the people'. An immediate consequence of these thoughts is that the phrase 'the people' should be proscribed in the discourse of democracy. It is a demagogue's term, a rhetorical expression merely which does not, because it cannot, mean what it says. It in fact applies only to a segment of the population, typically that segment constituting the enfranchised, however great or small a slice of the population this is, or (more usually in practice) that part of that slice of the population which voted for the victor's side of the argument.

In *The People and the Constitution* C. S. Emden writes, 'It has been remarked, with great authority, that "the people" is so indeterminate an expression that its use, let alone its abuse, obscures almost all political discussion. An even more absolute indictment is that of Disraeli, who once said that, as a political expression, "the people" is "sheer nonsense". He regarded it as belonging rather to the realm of natural history than to that of politics.'[3] The history of the phrase in the democratic era since Jefferson – and indeed, as a way of understanding the care attaching to his formulation: not 'the consent of the people' but 'the consent of the governed', the latter – 'the governed' – being everyone, and therefore the more inclusive concept, is instructive. Edmund Burke argued that 'the people' is a section of society characterized by having the ability, the opportunity and the information to engage in intelligent discussion of political matters. 'I have often endeavoured to compute and to class those who, in a political view, are to be called the people . . . In England and Scotland, I compute that those of adult age, not declining in life, of tolerable leisure for such discussions, and of some means of information, more or less, and who are above menial dependence, may amount to about four hundred thousand' (out of a population in Great Britain in the 1801 census of ten and a half million).[4]

This was a view shared by the proponents of electoral reform in the Great Reform Bill of 1832. Lord Brougham spoke of 'the well-informed and weighty parts of the community' as those whom the franchise should include; in debate on the Bill in Parliament itself he said, 'I do not mean the populace – the mob; I have never bowed to them, though I never have testified any unbecoming contempt of them . . . But, if there is a mob, there is a people also. I speak now of the middle classes – of those hundreds of thousands of respectable persons – the most numerous, and by far the most wealthy of the community.'[5] So out of the general population of 16.54 million in the 1831 census he identifies 'hundreds of thousands' of persons as 'the people', a minority he oddly describes as 'the most numerous' although they were assuredly 'by far the most wealthy' of the community.

An added complication in these usages is that the term 'the people' was also used to describe the generality of the population outside the upper classes. Viscount Canning indeed complained of this: '[he] protested against members of Parliament speaking of "the people" in contradistinction to the whole of the citizens. He regarded the people as incomplete without the aristocracy and gentry.'[6] This complaint is interesting: to that point 'the people' denoted by this usage had no vote, whereas those excluded from 'the people' did. The effect of the debates about democracy then having their first practical expression in electoral reform was to move the denotation of 'the people' from those without a political voice to those who had it or were, in the view of the reformers, worthy of it.

The operative distinction at stake, in being between *the enfranchised* and *the populace in general*, is best captured in an interesting characterization of it by the Abbé Sieyes. Sieyes' pamphlet 'What is the Third Estate?' was catalytic in the revolutionary events in France in the summer of 1789. In the previous year Louis XVI had called for a convocation of the Estates-General of France, these being the clergy (the First Estate), the nobility (the Second Estate) and the commoners (the Third Estate). It was the first time in a century and a half that the Estates had been convoked, and it gave Sieyes an opportunity to ask the question that inspired a revolution. He wrote, 'What is the Third Estate? Everything. What has it hitherto been in the political order? Nothing. What does it desire to be? Something.' This cry helped to transform the Estates-General into the National Assembly, for which Sieyes drafted the Declaration of the Rights of Man and the Citizen in which, among other matters of significance, he addressed the question of popular sovereignty and representation.

In doing so he distinguished between 'active citizens' and 'passive citizens', the former being those who have political rights in addition to their natural rights, the latter having natural rights only. He wrote, 'All inhabitants of a country should enjoy the rights of a passive citizen; all have a right to the protection of their persons, their property, their liberty and so on; but all have not the right to take part in the formation of public authority; all are not active citizens.' The choice of terminology is disagreeable; the idea of a 'passive' citizen carries the same paternalistic ring as use of the term 'the governed' in Jefferson's phrase, though it is even less appealing given that Jefferson emphasized the *consent* bestowed by the governed, whereas Sieyes speaks explicitly of 'passive' citizens not having the *right* to participate in 'forming public authority'.

But the underlying nuance of meaning is close. Consider Sieyes' rhetorical question and answer: 'What is a nation? A body of associates, living under a common law, and represented by the same legislature, etc.' The words 'represented by the same legislature' convey the same intention as the opening words of the Glorious Revolution's Bill of Rights (1688): 'the Lords Spiritual and Temporal and Commons assembled at Westminster lawfully fully and freely representing all the estates of the people of this realm'. Putting to one side time and language, what is in effect being claimed is that the functions of representing and consenting are correlative; the enfranchised (Sieyes' 'active' citizens) represent all the classes and interests of the whole populace, acceptance of which fact is assumed to convey, in the reverse direction, the consent of the governed.

There are two aspects to this. On the one hand, it is clearly not satisfactory to restrict the franchise in a minoritarian way. The argument for excluding substantial sections of the populace on grounds of education, property, sex, and age was a long sustained one; in the UK a property qualification was abolished at last only in 1918, women were only at last allowed to vote on the same terms as men in 1928, and the voting age was lowered from twenty-one to eighteen and with it the legal age of majority only in 1969. Note that each extension of the franchise in the UK between 1832 and 1969 was legislated in a 'Representation of the People Act', a phraseology consistent with the 1688 claim of the 'Lords Spiritual and Temporal and Commons' to represent *all* the 'estates of the people of this realm'. The claim to represent the people is by far not the same thing as the claim that the people are empowered with the authority of government.

And this is a key matter. If there were an intention to place sovereignty in the hands of the populace as a whole, or at least of all its adults however defined, it would need to be embodied in legislation called something like 'Empowerment of the People Act' or 'Sovereignty of the People Act'. But that has never been the intention of Parliament. In the UK's unwritten constitution the principle is that *Parliament* is sovereign, not the people, and successive extensions of the franchise have not disturbed that principle. Parliament represents the people in the sense that Parliament acts on their behalf; from its majority those who govern the people are drawn, and there is no power in the land – not the Crown, not the courts – which can overrule it, other than itself. This entails that extensions of the franchise have in effect been intended to make *consent* more explicit, by having more of the populace engaged in consciously giving that consent. Extensions of the franchise have not been intended to disperse *power* any more widely, except in what the outcome of an election does in settling which group in Parliament will form the government.

*   *   *

The failure of the institutional arrangements for the relationship between consent and government shows that there has to be constitutional reform or at least adjustment. Genuine reform in both the UK and US settings would be major and contentious, and could not be done without political courage. The present landscape offers no prospects of such a thing, only timidity or, as a substitute for courage, political bombast – extremists are always able to shout loudly and make wild threats and promises, whereas the political centre, if it is trying to conduct itself rationally and with practical ends in view, rarely generates the same heat and noise.

A process of constitutional reform has to start with consultation, debate, education, and analysis of proposed models and past experience. It has to be given time, and the process has itself to determine how consent for change is to be sought and given. In the ideal there would be consensus about the need for reform and the process by which it is achieved. There is never a better time to start a big project than now, for any now: there is no reason to delay.

Constitutional adjustment, as a more modest and more quickly achievable interim aim, is, however, a necessity. The current state of the democracies is unsustainable. The year 2016, with its Brexit and Trump phenomena and the anxieties prompted by both for important elections in Europe in 2017, show that the way the institutions and practices of democracy are being operated is a distortion of the intention that underlies them.

In the case of the UK the minimum required is that the electoral system should be changed so that it is more representative, and the system of political party discipline should be modified. Both points have already been made: I repeat them briefly for emphasis, as follows.

On the proportional representation point, one has to acknowledge that discussion of different electoral systems can wear thin the patience of saints. It is not necessary to discuss the technicalities of different approaches: it is needful only to say that a voting system which more closely approximates the spread of voter choice, but does not let in fringe or extremist elements with very small percentages of the vote, is the obvious requirement. The UK's first-past-the-post system is hopelessly unrepresentative, regularly producing governments with large majorities in the House of Commons on not much more than a third of total votes cast. That is simply unacceptable. Critics complain that voting reform would almost certainly result in coalition governments; the quickest response is to say that there is much to commend coalition governments.

The second point is crucial. As remarked above, one can justify 'whipping' the support of members of a parliamentary party from which the government is drawn when that government's election manifesto promises are at issue. But there is no justification for whipping a vote otherwise. Members of Parliament are representatives, acting on behalf of their own constituents and of the welfare of the nation at large. They are sent to Parliament to get information and listen to arguments, and on that basis to form judgments and decide what is in the best interests of the country, which would generally be the best interests of their constituents. Their independence in all matters unrelated to party manifesto commitments should be sacrosanct.

Theoretically the executive should be accountable to the legislature, not its owner; as things stand the relationship in the UK system of government is precisely that between a person and his dog. Greater independence for members of Parliament would place them in the position they should be in, monitoring the executive and holding it to account.

MPs should themselves be monitored and held to account by their constituents for their independence and observance of the duties of a parliamentarian. Their voters should be able to check their attendance, their interventions in debates, their voting record, their contribution to parliamentary committees, their constituency activities, their travel, visits, conferences, and meetings. I do not suggest that all constituents should be anxiously scrutinizing every minute of their MP's day; but they should be able to if they wish, and as election time approaches many of them should.

A state has a constitution, whether it is written or unwritten. It specifies the nature of the state's institutions, their duties, the extent and limit of their powers, the interrelationships between them, and the responsibilities of their officers. And it specifies the relationship between the state and its citizens.

In a written constitution these matters are codified, and means are provided for judicial review of whether the constitution's provisions are being properly applied. In an unwritten constitution these matters are regulated by custom and tradition, together with such statute as has been adopted to supplement or regularize the customs where changing conditions have made this necessary.

The virtues of a written constitution are clarity and definiteness. The virtue of an unwritten constitution is flexibility. The vices of each are the opposites of the opposite virtues. Critics of written constitutions point to the stipulative difficulty of amending the constitution. They cite the difficulties created by the way the US Constitution is treated as a piece of holy writ, and interpreted (think gun laws) in ways that are positively harmful to society. Critics of unwritten constitutions point to their vulnerability to changing interpretations from which there is no appeal, the changes prompted perhaps by expediency or partisanship.

An implication of these remarks is that a written constitution constrains government in ways that an unwritten constitution does not. The government is subject to it, whereas with an unwritten constitution it is the constitution which is subject to the government; the government can choose to alter it or interpret it in ways that suits itself. The UK is a remarkable case in point. A written constitution is therefore an important safeguard against abuses by government of its powers, not least because it would entrench civil liberties and the due processes of law.

This last is one of the chief considerations in favour of a written constitution. In the UK the Human Rights Act goes some way to entrenching citizens' liberties, but because it does not give the Supreme Court power to strike down legislation or restrain government action when either is at odds with the Act, the effect is not as powerful as a fully written constitution.

Those who say that a written constitution would be too rigid because amending it would be more onerous than amending or repealing statute law are in fact indicating a virtue: a constitution not at the whim of any current administration is a sterner guardian of rights and liberties than a constitution malleable to partisan and passing interests. Moreover, devising careful and consensual means for amending a constitution when changing circumstances make a powerful case for doing so cannot be beyond human ingenuity. The inflexibility of the US Constitution is the result of treating it as if it were scripture rather than a document serving a nation's needs; the problems of American governmental paralysis as a result of the bitter factionalism in its political life is a function of how difficult it is to reform itself. Written constitutions are a good thing except when they ossify into being a bad thing, and the United States illustrates why.

Those who say that an unwritten constitution allows democratic demand to shape the constitutional arrangements of the state, rather than vesting the power to interpret them in a Supreme Court, likewise miss an important point: that if constitutional change requires a supermajority in Parliament, or in a referendum, the change will be truly democratic, and will avoid the dangers pointed out by J. S. Mill as implicit in crude majoritarianism.

The argument that the UK's parliamentary sovereignty would be abolished by having a written constitution is intended to suggest that this would be a bad thing. In fact Parliament is not sovereign *de facto*; the executive is; this we have already seen. As the executive is drawn from the majority in Parliament, the whipping system of party discipline means that the executive is guaranteed to get its way, its party's members serving as lobby fodder to that end, in violation of the explicit duty of MPs to put the interests of their constituents and the country before all else – including before their party's interests. A constitutional duty otherwise, enforceable by judicial review, would go far to remedy the elective dictatorship – as Lord Hailsham put it – that results.

In any event, with an unwritten constitution and the putative sovereignty of Parliament, a single vote majority in the House of Commons can result in any violation of constitutional tradition or citizens' liberties, a degree of arbitrary power that is not acceptable in a diverse and complex modern society where most interests are minority interests and require protection.

CONCLUSION

In the Introduction I said that the political history of what we can call the 'Western liberal democracies' is the history of the development and application of a compromise aimed at resolving the dilemma of democracy – the dilemma of finding a way to locate the ultimate source of political authority in democratic assent, without democracy collapsing into mob rule or being hijacked by an oligarchy. To understand the compromise one must know that history. In Part I, I explained how the compromise emerged, and I offered some evaluation of it, and in Part II I explained the manner and causes of its breakdown in recent decades and especially in recent years; and then suggested a remedy – for as I said at the outset and repeat now, it is in my view unarguably right that the model of democracy forged by the compromise really is – as the Churchillian saying has it – by far the least bad of a lot of bad systems, which we would do well to preserve. I take the Churchillian phrase seriously: representative democracy is not perfect; but other forms of democracy, and all forms of non-democracy, are not as good, by quite a margin.

The motive for writing this book was the strong sense that the compromise in question, even though what one sees in the US and UK political orders are versions of that model only in appearance, has been inadequately applied, and this has reached a tipping point, exemplified by the election of Donald Trump in the United States and, in the United Kingdom, the Brexit referendum of June 2016 and the Conservative government's decision to treat its outcome as a mandate for taking the UK out of the European Union.

That Donald Trump was the least fit person ever to be elected to the White House is a widely shared view. He could have been stopped by 'faithless electors'[1] in the Electoral College, which had been invented precisely to keep unfit persons out of the White House; but by now the idea that this device of protection might actually be used is a dead letter. It was only ever once successfully used, to block the vice presidential nominee Richard M. Johnson in 1836, though since the promulgation of the US Constitution there have been 157 faithless electors in all. In 2016 four of the twelve electors in Washington State refused to vote for Hillary Clinton, who had officially won all twelve delegates; one of them voted for one of the activists opposing the Dakota pipeline, a person named Faith Spotted Eagle. Their reason was not to oppose Clinton but to persuade Republican electors to be faithless to Trump.

As an indication that the conditions for operating the American democracy are unfulfilled, it is educative to read the Trump-supporting essay 'The Flight 93 Election', whose author chose the pseudonym 'Publius Decius Mus'. Regarded as an influential blast from the alt-right, it claimed to provide intellectual support for Donald Trump's candidacy, though in substance it is little more than a slasher piece offering the standard complaint that the liberal left in America is responsible for immigration, high taxes, big government, the failure of schools to educate, overseas wars, and the 'Macarthyism' of Political Correctness (for which read conservative dislike of affirmative attitudes to women and minorities – however true it is that 'PC' has gone far too far, and it has, its origins in these respects remain valid). 'Mus' argued instead for the familiar conservative litany of family values, religion, business, low taxes, morality, schools to inculcate 'good character,' and so forth. His point was that not even the Republican Party version of conservatism is enough to save the US from going over a cliff, and therefore the country needs a shake-up for which 'Trump's vulgarity is a godsend' – though the author's view of Trump as vulgar is not to the point, for he applauds Trump's hostility to immigration, globalization, and assorted other conservative *bêtes noires*.

The author's premise – that the United States is in dire trouble – is false except from the point of view of one who would like to put women and minorities back in their boxes, schoolchildren to be obedient, government to be small, and the population white. But insofar as it is in enough trouble, even if not dire, it is because the political structures have been hijacked to make them all check and no balance; the factionalism Madison strove to avoid has paralysed it. A study by Martin Gilens and Benjamin Page puts the point robustly: 'the US', they say, 'is no longer a democracy.'[2] One of their chief reasons is that the first-past-the-post voting system in gerrymandered congressional districts results in representation in the House of Representatives failing to be representative. Another is the unrepresentative nature of the Senate, each state, however populous or unpopulous, returning two senators. A third reason is that a Supreme Court ruling allows billionaires to give unlimited amounts of money to campaigns at all levels; political office in the US is bought and sold like pairs of socks.

Suggestions from US commentators on the failings of the Constitution include arguing for greater presidential powers. In *Relic: How the Constitution Undermines Effective Government* William Howell and Terry Moe argue that the Constitution makes Congress 'irresponsible and ineffective' and too tied to parochial pork-barrel issues in their districts solely for the purpose of re-election.[3] The failure of Congress to be a fully functional seat of legislation permeates through the rest of the system, they argue, whose checks and balances too are powerful in respect of checks and too unbalanced to make effective government possible. Other remedies for the same complaint are legion.

The UK's Brexit referendum is another example of failure. There are strong grounds for regarding both the referendum and the subsequent government actions as politically illegitimate and constitutionally unsound: I set out the case for this in the Appendix.[4] Dismay at the flaccidity of the political order, which had but did not apply the tools to deal with the problem, was itself a prompt to this examination of the matter.

And that is where returning to the source comes in. In the writings of Aristotle, Locke, Montesquieu, Madison, Constant, de Tocqueville and Mill, among others, the idea of a democratic order adequate to the meliorist task of transforming the endorsement of a *demos* into stable government is clearly developed. To say that these ideas offer the best resolution to the dilemma of democracy is, as we see, not to say that regimes such as those operative in the UK and the US need no reform; indeed, to implement these ideas requires that obstacles to doing so should be removed by such reform. In the UK there is a second chamber and an independent judiciary; yet the executive is supreme and unstoppable, and the putative checks on its power are impotent. In the US the opposite problem obtains;

the checks are so used and abused as to make governing ineffective. Cleaving to the intention of the theoreticians of representative democracy would pull both systems back from the distorted and dysfunctional versions of that intention that they have now become.

The point just made addresses the internal corrosion of the political orders themselves in the UK and the US. To say that the ideas of Madison, Constant and the rest offer the best resolution to the dilemma of democracy is not to say that these democracies need be unconcerned about the other threats posed to them and their populaces by the less savoury ambitions of big business, big money, vested interests, international interests, the sphere of private profit and partisan action, and interference by unfriendly governments. On the contrary: if anything is to be meant by 'sound' government it is government for the good of all, and serious questions are raised about the functioning of the order if populist disquiet is aroused by feelings of marginalization and irrelevance. Part of that disquiet is the result of leaving 'the market' and private acquisitiveness to determine aspects of human relationships, with the bottom line of the balance sheet taking precedence over the needs and interests of human individuals. Unjust inequalities, and inequalities legitimately caused but too great, are toxic to a society; inclusion and a fair distribution of opportunities for access to social goods and participation are minimal requirements of a good society, to be served by sound government – which means not just stable but just, enabling, considerate, inclusive government. The idea here is that the institutions and practices proposed as a resolution to the dilemma of democracy would, if fully applied with transparency in a constitutional order where the rights and liberties of citizens are guaranteed, be a democracy of and for all the people where 'the people' literally means everyone.

The one point that by way of conclusion merits yet a further iteration is the idea of the education of the *demos* to make it approximate more to what a democracy needs in order really to flourish. There are two aspects to this. One is that the population of a democratic state should understand the state's politics and structures of government, should have a grown-up sense of what politics and government can and cannot do, and should have access to reliable information on which to base its own participation, in debate and at the ballot box, in the processes of the democratic order. These are things that society itself can seek to achieve, by means of the school curriculum and in demanding that the media should be responsible.

The other is considerably harder to achieve, on the grounds that one can do no more than take a horse to water. This is that the great majority of members of the *demos* would themselves become the individuals that a democratic order longs to be populated by – the opposite of those disparaged by Plato and others as unsuited to the role democracy needs them to play. Pessimism on this head is near universal; and one would wish to object that it is a calumny on the human species. It is extremely hard not to agree with Madison that realism and practicality oblige one to focus on the institutions and practices of democracy to seek a remedy. While that is so, his suggestions, and those of others in the tradition of debate that produced the concept of representative democracy, are not only the best we have, but they are good.

Or they would be, if properly applied.

So, to sum up: there are simple and direct remedies that would go a long way to rescuing representative democracy from the distortions and manipulations it has been subjected to.

186

There should be complete transparency about which individuals and organizations are involved in election campaigning, on what basis and by what methods.

There should be complete transparency about the funding involved in an election campaign, not just in the period of the campaign itself but in the research and development of all methods used in campaigning; and a cap on it.

The press should be subject to strict fact-check monitoring, and stiff fines levied for purveying deliberate misinformation.

Betting on the outcome of elections should be banned, and polling should cease for a period before voting takes place.

Voting should be compulsory for all citizens, and the voting age should be sixteen. Civic education on the political and governmental system should be obligatory in schools for pupils aged fourteen and above.

In both the UK and US settings, replacement of the first-past-the-post electoral system with an adequate proportional representation system is essential.

Also essential is reform of the party discipline system in the UK to make it impermissible to apply the whip to MPs for matters other than election manifesto commitments.

These last two provisions alone would restore the British parliamentary system to something closer to the intention behind its structure, and would end the 'elective dictatorship' of the executive.

With these essentials in place, representative democracy has a chance of working – to everyone's benefit. In some countries with systems of representative democracy some of these provisions already exist, much to their credit. But all are at risk from what happened in 2016 in the EU referendum in the UK and the US presidential election. The year 2016 deserves to stand as the moment when at last the question of what has happened to the system of representative democracy requires thorough examination and overhaul, in the interests of preserving it as the best system for ensuring that government is based on 'the consent of the people' and genuinely represents the people's best interests.

APPENDIX I

BREXIT

The Brexit referendum on 23 June 2016 is an example of how the constitutional and political order of the UK is in a highly questionable state. Without overexaggerating, it is arguable that the EU referendum itself and the government's subsequent actions resemble something like a coup – a strong claim; but allow the following details to speak for themselves.

The EU membership referendum franchise excluded – after discussion of the matter prior to introduction of the EU Referendum Bill in Parliament – sixteen- and seventeen-year-olds, expatriate British citizens who had lived abroad for more than a certain number of years, and EU citizens resident in the UK and paying their taxes there. It would seem obvious that all three groups should have been included as having the most material interest in the outcome of the vote. In the franchise for the Scottish independence referendum of 2014, sixteen- and seventeen-year-olds had the vote and so did EU citizens resident in Scotland. No threshold was specified for the outcome of the referendum, unlike the 1979 Scottish devolution referendum which required that 40% of the entire electorate should be in favour for any change to take place. In Briefing Paper 07212 published on 3 June 2015 all MPs and members of the House of Lords were told that the referendum was advisory only, and would not be binding on Parliament or government. This point was iterated *viva voce* by the Minister for Europe in the debate in the House of Commons later that month. This was the reason given for not including a threshold and for not extending the franchise appropriately.

The outcome was that 37% of the restricted electorate given the franchise for the referendum voted to leave the EU. This outcome is by any standards insufficient to justify a constitutional change so significant as the UK's exiting the EU. There is scarcely any civilized state in the world where a simple majority, let alone a small one, would permit this: for such a change, a supermajority would be required, of 60% or 66% either of votes cast or the entire electorate. Yet a small minority of actual votes cast, representing 37% of the total electorate, was taken by the politicians in favour of Brexit as not merely justifying but mandating the actions they took following the referendum. There is therefore nowhere near enough justification or legitimacy for a Brexit.[1]

The Brexit ministry empanelled after the referendum sought to trigger Article 50 of the Lisbon Treaty notifying EU partners of an intention to leave the EU, without a parliamentary debate. It had to be taken to court to oblige it to respect the constitutional sovereignty of Parliament. In response, and arguably in contempt both of what is meant to be Parliament's role and of the intention of the Supreme Court judgment, the government introduced a very short Bill of a few lines to hasten through Parliament, with restricted time to discuss it, and a full three-line whip to ensure that its own MPs, whatever their real views, would vote for triggering Article 50 despite any argument, facts, considerations or warnings that might come up in the hurried debate.

The purport of Briefing Paper 07212 issued to members of both Houses of Parliament on 3 June 2015 in advance of debate on the Referendum Bill returns to relevance here. It says in section 5 that the referendum is non-binding, advisory, consultative; and section 6 points out that if there were to be any suggestion otherwise, there would need to be a supermajority requirement. In the House of Commons in the debate on the EU Referendum Bill the Minister for Europe, David Lidington, told the House that 'the legislation is about holding a vote; it makes no provision for what follows. The referendum is advisory' (Hansard for 16 June 2015). Yet the Brexit ministry has chose to treat the referendum outcome as binding and mandating, in defiance of the explicit nature of the Referendum Act itself. This and the inconsistencies of this referendum with other referenda raise a serious question of constitutional propriety. To arrange things as convenient for a given occasion – in effect making them up as one goes along – without any question of conformity to a due process and a propriety of constitutional order, throws the legitimacy of the process into doubt. This applies in a major way to the EU referendum in 2016.

It is relevant to recall that the 2016 EU referendum was not necessitated by any crisis in the EU or in the UK's relations with its EU partners; there were no threats or problems arising from EU membership, other than those alleged (and alleged for over forty years of anti-EU activism) by 'Eurosceptics' and politicians on the right of the Conservative Party and UKIP. It was in fact an effort by the then leadership of the Conservative Party to stifle temporarily a long-standing quarrel within that party. During the previous coalition government David Cameron promised a referendum, against the advice of his senior colleagues, to silence the far right of his party, which was engaged in its usual procedure of making life difficult as they had done for every Conservative Prime Minister since 1972.

Cameron almost certainly did not expect to win the election of 2015, still less with an outright majority. He had offered the referendum as one might offer a bone to quieten barking dogs. When he won a majority in the election, he was obliged to honour the promise. Neither he nor anyone else, including the pro-Brexit camp, expected Leave to 'win', so he culpably allowed the Brexit faction to arrange the franchise in a way that best suited them – this being the exclusion of sixteen- to seventeen-year-olds (Cameron subsequently said that insisting on their inclusion would have caused too much trouble with his right wing), expatriates, and EU taxpayers in the UK, who between them would have assured a significant Remain majority, a fact the Brexiters well understood. Deliberate restriction of the franchise is gerrymandering: the EU referendum was gerrymandered.

Likewise no one asked the Brexiters to produce an account of what would follow if a Leave vote won: there were no details, no manifesto, only one apparent promise – the EU subvention to be dedicated to the NHS at the rate of £350 million per week – and otherwise a raft of misleading claims and false statements and slogans, as the next section shows.

In the absence of any detail on what a Brexit would mean or involve, months after the referendum, months after the Supreme Court case, and indeed *after* the debate on the Article 50 Bill in the House of Commons, a White Paper on Brexit was published, consisting of a hurried re-edit of some of Prime Minister May's speeches. It does, however, contain two points of interest. One is dealt with in the next section below, concerning the matter of the 'sovereignty' of the UK. The other is the extraordinary statement that all sixty-five million citizens of the UK were fully behind Brexit. I mention this because of the question of 'representation' discussed earlier, where 'representation' does not always mean direct electoral representation. In this connection, therefore, it is of relevance that it is in the public domain that seventeen million voted for Brexit, sixteen million opposed it, and thirty-two million did not vote. The Prime Minister's claim was therefore Orwellian Newspeak, and involved dismissing the concerns, interests and stated preferences of nearly half the people who voted in the referendum, and of all who could not vote and did not vote. Together with the questionable considerations about the nature and validity of the referendum itself, the EU referendum and its subsequent use by the government is profoundly unrepresentative, and therefore constitutionally improper.

The falsity of the claim that the whole country is behind Brexit is further demonstrated by Scotland, Northern Ireland and Gibraltar, whose choice and interests had been ignored by the Brexit ministry: all three voted emphatically to Remain. Scotland was thereby given full moral justification to seek to leave the UK, and Northern Ireland is faced with an agonizing problem over the Good Friday Agreement and its land border with the Irish Republic. The blame for dismemberment of the UK, and for a resumption of tensions and difficulties that membership of the EU has done so much to overcome, will lie with the Brexit government's use of the referendum as an excuse for its policy of exiting the EU.

To summarise so far: the referendum was gerrymandered and badly designed; it was the result of an internal Conservative Party squabble; it exposes the Brexit ministry's contempt for Parliament and people as shown by its being obliged by the courts to consult Parliament; it was careless of the unity of the UK and the concerns of the UK's different peoples and inter-ests – all this, together with what is noted in the next section about the nature of the Leave campaign, strongly indicates that there is no political legitimacy for, and no political rationality in, the major constitutional change Brexit involves.

Proponents of Brexit constantly iterated the 'will of the people' claim: more Newspeak, for the basis of their claim is only 37% of the electorate, which represents 26% of 'the people' if this phrase means the population of the UK. But even if you allow 37% of a gerrymandered electorate to be 'the people' for a moment: were this 37% of one mind in voting Leave? Did they all want to leave the EU for the same reasons? Did they have a clear idea, involving practical details, of what would follow? No. Compare them to the Remainers, all of whom wanted the same thing, a thing they were perfectly familiar with because they had had it for over forty years: membership of the EU and member-ship's many benefits. Earlier the use of hidden manipulative techniques for aggregating disparate constituencies of voters was discussed; one requirement for a functioning constitutional order is complete transparency of all methods used to put forward a political programme for consideration by the elector-ate. This rational and proper requirement was violated in this case on a very significant scale.

The Leave referendum campaign contained one and only one apparent promise: that the money the UK pays into the common budget of the EU would go instead to the NHS, in the order of £350 million per week. The major risk to the UK economy of withdrawal from the EU had been made clear by the Remain campaign. A smaller GDP and increased costs to every aspect of British economic life were forewarned by the experts whom Michael Gove – a former Secretary of State for education, note – dismissed with contempt. Politicians on the Leave side said that a UK outside the EU would be able to become a low-tax deregulated economy, inviting to businesses not keen to bear the burden of employer and consumer protections and environmental controls on their activities, and keen to benefit from low rates of taxation. Such an economy does not have resources for a national health service, a good state education service, a welfare net, and environmental protections – none of which are of interest to wealthy people who make use of private health and education, will never need welfare, and take their holidays abroad on other people's clean beaches.

But leave aside the '£350 million a week to the NHS' promise, the immediate breaking of which appears to be too remarkably egregious a matter for those who made it – Boris Johnson and others – to be held accountable for it. Look at two key issues used to get a Leave vote: claims about 'sovereignty' and claims about immigration.

The White Paper itself exposes the untruth about sovereignty. It says in reference to the 'take back control' slogan of the Leave campaign: 'The sovereignty of Parliament is a fundamental principle of the UK constitution. Whilst Parliament has remained sovereign throughout our membership of the EU, it has not always felt like that' (section 2.1 Cm 9417). To repeat: the UK has always been sovereign, but (says the White Paper) it has '*not always felt like that*'. This section of the White Paper is entitled 'Taking control of our own laws'. There is no mention of the fact that the UK not only agreed to 95% of all EU laws but initiated many of them. We read in the White Paper that 'the sovereignty of Parliament is a fundamental principle of the UK constitution' and yet the government treats 37% of a gerrymandered electorate as sovereign, usurping and trumping the sovereignty of Parliament by forbidding it to treat an advisory referendum as advisory. These inconsistencies are evidence of Brexit proponents' cavalier treatment of political and constitutional proprieties.

One notes that the White Paper was finished at 4.07 am in the morning *after* the debate in the House of Commons on triggering Article 50; White Papers are intended to provide information, and an assessment of options, *before* debate on a Bill in Parliament. This adds to the serious question about the political legitimacy and constitutional propriety of the entire EU referendum and post-referendum proceedings.

The same concerns apply to claims made about immigration in the Leave campaign. Let us simply acknowledge that anti-immigrant sentiment has too much in it of xenophobia and racism, that it is based not merely on ignorance of what immigrants provide to the country – for example, 26% of NHS staff, net contributions to the tax base, much needed labour in agriculture, vigour to the economy – and note that one immediate result of Brexit might be *increased* immigration (as reported in the *Guardian*, 3 February 2017). The UK economy needs immigrants, and the immigrants who make their homes here put more into the economy than they take out. Promoting anti-immigrant sentiment is disgraceful in its own right, but it is doubly so when based on deliberate misinformation about the effect of their presence in the economy. Here the decades of falsehood and propaganda from the *Daily Mail*, *Daily Express*, the *Sun*, the Conservative right wing, and its ideological outer arm UKIP have done a grave disservice.

In noting that each of the key themes of the Leave campaign – money for the NHS, sovereignty, immigration – has been withdrawn or shown to be incorrect since the referendum, we have to ask why the political haste towards taking the UK out of the EU continues unabated. Questions of political integrity therefore arise.

All these points illustrate how a major political event in the UK exposes the sham of the constitutional arrangements, so easily and readily manipulable by the executive for highly partisan ends, however damaging to the polity and populace as a whole. No constitutional system should allow a partisan group to hijack the interests of the whole: this is happening in the UK and the US as these words are being written. This is not what the architects of representative democracy intended, and it is fundamentally against the interests of the people of those countries. It is therefore a matter of urgency to return our advanced polities to their democratic roots.

APPENDIX II

THE FAILURE OF
DEMOCRACY ELSEWHERE

'Democracy' became a feel-good word in the twentieth century. Not only did non-democracies take to calling themselves 'the Democratic Republic of This' or 'the People's Republic of That', as already noted, but in fact or in aspiration over half the world's states had become electoral democracies by 2010. This contrasts with the fact that before 1970 only a third of the world's states were so. It is surprising now to remember that in 1970 Greece, Spain and Portugal were dictatorships, as were most South American countries; the Soviet bloc was still powerful, and the prospect of newly independent former colonies and protectorates in Africa did not look as if they would adhere to the democratic principles that departing colonial masters had attempted to construct as they left.

The Western liberal democracies looked like shining beacons in contrast, and their success in economic and military respects offered the rest of the world a model which had a great deal to do with the number of countries adopting the lineaments of democracy during the remaining decades of the century. It is, however, questionable whether this move to emulate the Western democracies will continue now that another model offers itself – the Chinese model, in which tight political control is maintained while economic liberalization roars ahead. For the rulers in some developing states it must be tempting indeed to think that one could remain permanently in government, quelling opposition and denying civil liberties, while the economy grows at 10% per annum.

The chief difference between the Chinese and Western political models lies in the fact that the former is greatly more efficient than the latter. In the Chinese model there is no debate and discussion outside the Politburo, no changes of direction following elections – in general, none of the uncertainty and delay that electoral politics brings. Democracy is cumbersome from the point of view of a country that wants to advance very rapidly in economic terms, not troubling itself overmuch with employee protection, care of the environment, and regulations and red tape, especially given that much of the latter changes with changing governments. What democracy offers in return for its cumbersome inefficiency is civil liberties and the involvement of the enfranchised part of the population in legitimizing government. These are precious possessions, not lightly to be given up.

As Francis Fukuyama shows in his *Origins of Political Order*, the high tide of democratization in the world – so far anyway – seems to have occurred at the end of the last decade of the twentieth century.[1] He cites examples of states reversing the democratic gains they had made, such as Russia, Iran and Venezuela; of states stuck in what has been called a 'grey zone' between autocracy and semi-democracy, such as Uzbekistan and Kazakhstan; of states which despite acquiring democratic institutions have not delivered sound and stable government, such as Ukraine. From Bolivia to India corruption and yawning inequality are endemic. Repeated economic crises in an unstable globalized order are a symptom of political failure at regulating the activities of markets, not least financial markets. All these considerations raise questions about democracy, its effectiveness, its current state, and its future.

The very various experiences of democracy in different parts of the world, and questions about its resilience or otherwise in the face of global economic pressures and internal social challenges, would be a subject very worthy of study. Were this a different kind of book, this comparative task would be relevant. But it is not the ambition here to make a general comparison of this kind, though a valuable consequence of doing so would be to identify the places where representative democracy has not been undermined by big money, Big Data campaigning techniques, anti-democratic party discipline structures that institutionalize factionalism, and other causes of decay. The task here has been to focus just on the two salient cases of what the Trump election and the Brexit referendum show about the state of democracy in those two polities. The diagnosis in these cases suggests the cure – which includes complete transparency of all the players and methods in campaigns, limits on campaign finance, proper operation of the institutions of the democratic order as they are intended to be operated, and limits on the degree of party discipline outside manifesto commitments.

The importance of mentioning this does not arise only from the fact that the democratic orders in the US and the UK have become so manipulated as to produce the shocks of 2016. There is an even more general problem. This is that when highly partisan governments secure power by such means, they give freedom to other partisan interests to operate at the expense of the rest of society. The point has been well made by George Monbiot in *How Did We Get Into This Mess?* Capture of the political process by a highly partisan group means that it frees itself and its supporters (and funders) from the controls that the democratic order exists to impose in the interests of both minorities and the collective; for, he says, they give themselves 'freedom from the demands of social justice, from environmental constraints, from collective bargaining and from the taxation that funds public services. It means, in sum, freedom from democracy.'[2]

Subverted democracy, in short, is no democracy; a political order which is meant to translate democratic preferences into sound government, but where the preferences have been manipulated and the government is operated in the interests of only one part of the populace, is not a democratic political order. This, as the body of this book argues, is the situation in the US and the UK of today.

BIBLIOGRAPHY

Christopher Achen and Larry Bartels, *Democracy for Realists* (Princeton: Princeton University Press, 2016)

Aristotle, *Politics*, trans. Benjamin Jowett (1885)

A. Aspinall, *Lord Brougham and the Whig Party* (London: Nonsuch Publishing, 2005)

Francis Bacon, *The Advancement of Learning* (Halcyon Press 2009)

Deborah Baumgold, *Hobbes's Political Theory* (Cambridge: Cambridge University Press, 1988)

Karel Beckman and Frank Karsten, *Beyond Democracy* (CreateSpace Independent Publishing Platform, 2012)

Ricardo Blaug, *Democracy: A Reader* (Edinburgh: Edinburgh University Press, 2nd ed., 2016)

Jacques-Bénigne Bossuet, ed. Patrick Riley, *Politics Drawn from the Very Words of Holy Scripture* (Cambridge: Cambridge University Press, 1990, 1999)

Jason Brennan, *Against Democracy* (Princeton: Princeton University Press, 2016)

Wendy Brown, *Undoing the Demos* (Cambridge, Mass: MIT Press, 2015)

Edmund Burke, Speech to the Electors of Bristol (3 November 1774), *Works 1*, pp. 446–48

Paul Cartledge, *Democracy: A Life* (Oxford: Oxford University Press, 2016)

Benjamin Constant, *The Liberty of the Ancients Compared with that of the Moderns* (1819)

Bernard Crick, *Democracy* (Oxford: Oxford University Press, 2002)

Robert A. Dahl, *Democracy and Its Critics* (New Haven: Yale University Press, 1991)

—*On Democracy* (New Haven: Yale University Press, 2000)

John Dryzek and Patrick Dunleavy, *Theories of the Democratic State* (London: Palgrave Macmillan, 2009)

John Dunn, *Setting the People Free* (London: Atlantic Books, 2006)

C. S. Emden, *The People and the Constitution* (Oxford: Oxford University Press, 2nd ed., 1956)

Francis Fukuyama, *The Origins of Political Order* (London: Profile Books, 2011)

David Gauthier, *The Logic of Leviathan* (Oxford: Clarendon Press, 1979)

Martin Gilens and Benjamin L. Page, 'Testing Theories of American Politics: Elites, Interest Groups, and Average Citizens', *Perspectives on Politics*, Volume 12, Issue 3, September 2014

Jean Hampton, *Hobbes and the Social Contract Tradition* (Cambridge: Cambridge University Press, 1986)

David Held, *Models of Democracy* (Oxford: Polity Press, 3rd ed., 2006)

Christopher Hill, *The World Turned Upside Down: Radical Ideas During the English Revolution* (London: Penguin, 1991)

Thomas Hobbes, *Leviathan*, Clarendon Edition of the Works of Thomas Hobbes Volume 1 (Oxford: Clarendon Press, 2012)

—*Behemoth*, Clarendon Edition of the Works of Thomas Hobbes Volume 10 (Oxford: Clarendon Press, 2014)

Quintin Hogg, Lord Hailsham, 'Elective Dictatorship', The Richard Dimbleby Lecture, *The Listener*, 21 October 1976

William G. Howell and Terry M. Moe, *Relic: How the Constitution Undermines Effective Government* (New York: Basic Books, 2016)

Thomas Jefferson, Declaration of Independence, 1776

Daniel Kahneman, *Thinking Fast and Slow* (London: Penguin, 2011)

John Keane, *The Life and Death of Democracy* (London: Simon and Schuster, 2010)

Arend Lijphart, *Patterns of Democracy* (New Haven: Yale University Press, 1999)

John Locke, *Two Treatises of Government* (Cambridge: Cambridge University Press, 1988)

Niccolo Machiavelli, *The Prince*, trans. George Bull (London: Penguin Classics, 2003)

Charles Mackay, *Extraordinary Popular Delusions and the Madness of Crowds* (1841)

BIBLIOGRAPHY

James Madison, *The Federalist Papers*, No. 10, 22 November 1787

John Stuart Mill, *Considerations on Representative Government* (1861)

George Monbiot, *How Did We Get Into This Mess?* (London: Verso, 2016)

Baron de Montesquieu, *The Spirit of the Laws*, trans. Anne Cohler, Basia Miller, Harold Stone (Cambridge: Cambridge University Press, 1989)

Carole Pateman, *Participation and Democratic Theory* (Cambridge: Cambridge University Press, 1970)

Plato, *The Republic*, trans. Benjamin Jowett (1894)

A. F. Pollard, *The Evolution of Parliament* (London: Longmans Green & Co., 2nd ed., revised ed., 1926)

Polybius, *Histories*, trans. W. R. Paton (Cambridge, Mass: Harvard University Press, 1922)

Putney Debates full transcript:

press-pubs.uchicago.edu/founders/print_documents/v1ch15s1.html

Michael Rosen and Jonathan Wolff, *Political Thought* (Oxford: Oxford University Press, 1999)

Jean-Jacques Rousseau, *The Social Contract*, trans. Maurice Cranston (London: Penguin Classics, 1968)

Joseph Schumpeter, *Capitalism, Socialism and Democracy* (London: George Allen & Unwin Ltd, 1943)

Quentin Skinner, *Liberty before Liberalism* (Cambridge: Cambridge University Press, 1998)

—*Visions of Politics: Volume III: Hobbes and Civil Science* (Cambridge: Cambridge University Press, 2002)

Baruch Spinoza, *Tractatus Theologico-Politicus*, trans. R. H. M. Elwes (London: Routledge, 1914). Full text available online

Thucydides, *The History of the Peloponnesian War*, trans. Benjamin Jowett (1881)

Alexis de Tocqueville, *Democracy in America* (1831), trans. G. Bevan (London: Penguin Classics, 2003)

Tzvetan Todorov, *The Inner Enemies of Democracy*, trans. Andrew Brown (Oxford: Polity Press, 2014)

Nadine Urbinati, *Mill on Democracy* (Chicago: Chicago University Press, 2002)

NOTES

Introduction

1 Hansard, 11 November 1947.
2 One could quote Francis Bacon here: 'From moral virtue let us pass on to matter of power and commandment, and consider whether in right reason there be any comparable with that wherewith knowledge investeth and crowneth man's nature. We see the dignity of the commandment is according to the dignity of the commanded; to have commandment over beasts as herdmen have, is a thing contemptible; to have commandment over children as schoolmasters have, is a matter of small honour; to have commandment over galley-slaves is a disparagement rather than an honour. Neither is the commandment of tyrants much better, over people which have put off the generosity of their minds; and, therefore, it was ever holden that honours in free monarchies and commonwealths had a sweetness more than in tyrannies, because the commandment extendeth more over the wills of men, and not only over their deeds and services.' *The Advancement of Learning* VIII (3).
3 The phrase 'the madness of crowds' is from Charles Mackay, *Extraordinary Popular Delusions and the Madness of Crowds* (1841).
4 This immediately prompts questions about social media, the blogosphere, 'post-truth' and 'alternative facts', fake news, and how reliable information and serious analysis and debate can be maintained.

5 The cost of resort to law in practice subverts this principle.

6 To describe this as a 'coup' might literally be correct; see later in these pages what Locke says about the right of the people to resist a government that behaves in this kind of way, and Mill's discussion of 'constitutional morality' which supports that case.

1 The History of the Dilemma Part I:
Plato, Aristotle, Machiavelli

1 Plato's views are to be found in *The Republic* Book VIII. The translation used here is by Benjamin Jowett (1894).

2 The chief source for Aristotle's views is *Politics* Books III and IV. The translation used here is by Benjamin Jowett (1885).

3 Pericles' funeral oration from Thucydides, *The History of the Peloponnesian War* Book 2. The translation used here is by Benjamin Jowett (1881).

4 Wikipedia 'List of revolutions and rebellions' https://en.wikipedia.org/wiki/List_of_revolutions_and_rebellions#BC.

5 Critics of the 'dynastic cycles' theory point out that it complicates understanding of China's history because it distorts near-contemporary records of events.

6 'Heaven' is not a religious concept, although it might be describable as a superstitious one. There is no God in Chinese thought. Ancestor worship, a mythology of 'Immortals', and a lively and fearful belief in ghosts, demonstrates the traditional Chinese belief in an afterlife.

7 Polybius, *Histories* Book VI. The translation used here is by W. R. Paton (1922).

8 Ulpianus, *The Digest of Justinian* 1. 4. 1, trans. C. H. Monro (Cambridge: Cambridge University Press, 1904).

9 This and subsequent quotations are from Niccolo Machiavelli, The Harvard Classics (1909–14), available online: http://www.bartleby.com/36/1/prince.pdf and *Docucu* archive http://www.docucu-archive.com/view/6e3161eb6e24b653adf800bbc61513f6/Discourses-Machiavelli.pdf.

10 Not long after Bhutan was made a democracy – against the will of its people! – by King Jigme Singye Wangchuck, the United Nations Development Account invited a number of academics and writers to participate in a conference at Paro on the idea of a democratic order. My contribution to the discussion was the idea that whereas the sound of

tyranny is silence, democracy is noisy, strident and argumentative; and that this is a good thing. The point is in essentials Machiavelli's, at least as regards the important matter of giving everyone a voice. It is only one aspect of ensuring that the result is not ochlocratic.

2 The History of the Dilemma Part II: The Putney Debates, 1647

1 The full text may be read at https://en.wikisource.org/wiki/ An_Agreement_of_the_People_(1647).

3 The Beginnings of a Solution Part I: Locke, Hobbes, Spinoza

1 Jacques-Bénigne Bossuet, *Politics Drawn from the Very Words of Holy Scripture* (1990, 1999).
2 Ibid.
3 Thomas Hobbes, *Leviathan*, Part II, Of Commonwealth, Chapter 17.
4 Ibid.
5 Op. cit., Chapter 18.
6 Ibid.
7 Op. cit., Chapter 30.
8 Scholars debate whether this is so. See Jean Hampton, *Hobbes and the Social Contract Tradition* (1986); David Gauthier, *The Logic of Leviathan* (1979); Deborah Baumgold, *Hobbes's Political Theory* (1988).
9 John Locke, *The Second Treatise of Government*, Chapter 1, section 4.
10 Op. cit., Chapter 1, section 6.
11 Op. cit., Chapter 4, section 23.
12 Op. cit., Chapter 11, section 135.
13 Op. cit., Chapter 19, section 240.
14 Op. cit., Chapter 10, section 143.
15 Op. cit., Chapter 19, sections 155, 207, 220–31.
16 Not in the pejorative sense employed by the American political right wing, for whom 'liberal' is a surrogate for 'socialist', both terms of malediction in their lexicon.
17 Hobbes, *Behemoth*, p. 75.
18 Baruch Spinoza, *Tractatus Theologico-Politicus*, pp. 9, 14.
19 Hobbes, *Behemoth*, p. 16.

20 Hobbes, *Leviathan*, Part I, Of Man, Chapter 10.
21 The Marxist historian and Master of Balliol College, Oxford, Christopher Hill, regarded the English Civil War as the first of the great revolutions of modern Western history, precipitating by a (slow) chain reaction those in the American colonies, France in 1789, the European uprisings of 1830 and 1848, the nineteenth century's South American revolutions, and the Russian revolutions of 1917.

4 The Beginnings of a Solution Part II: Montesquieu, Rousseau

1 Baron de Montesquieu, *The Spirit of the Laws*, Book III, Chapter 3, 'Of the Principle of Democracy'.
2 Ibid.
3 Op. cit., Book IV, Chapter 3, 'Of Education in a Republican Government'.
4 Op. cit., Book VIII, Chapter 2, 'Of the Corruption of the Three Governments'.
5 Op. cit., Book XI, Chapter 4, 'The Same Subject [Liberty] Continued'.
6 Rousseau, *The Social Contract*, Book IV, Chapter 1.
7 Op. cit., Book II, Chapter 3.
8 Ibid.
9 Rousseau, op. cit., Book III, Chapter 4.

5 Solutions Proposed Part I: Madison, Constant

1 The Virginia Declaration of Rights, Thomas Mason, 1776.
2 Declaration of Independence, Thomas Jefferson, 1776.
3 James Madison, *The Federalist Papers*, No. 10, 22 November 1787.
4 John Adams, Letter to John Taylor, 17 December 1814.
5 James Madison, *The Federalist Papers*, No. 10, 22 November 1787.
6 Ibid.
7 Ibid.
8 Ibid.
9 Ibid.
10 Ibid.
11 Ibid.
12 Ibid.
13 Ibid.

14 Benjamin Constant, *The Liberty of the Ancients Compared with that of the Moderns* (1819).

15 Ibid.

16 Ibid.

17 The honourable exception, which Constant acknowledges, is the Athens especially of the Periclean democracy: see the funeral oration of Pericles quoted in Chapter 2 above.

18 Constant, op. cit.

19 Ibid.

20 Ibid.

21 Ibid.

22 Ibid.

6 Solutions Proposed Part II: De Tocqueville, Mill

1 Alexis de Tocqueville, *Democracy in America* (1831), Introductory chapter.

2 Ibid.

3 Op. cit., Book II, Chapter 6.

4 Op. cit., Book I, Chapter 10.

5 Op. cit., Book I, Chapter 3, pt. 1.

6 Op. cit., Book I, Chapter 5.

7 Op. cit., Book II, Chapter 5.

8 Ibid.

9 Ibid.

10 Ibid.

11 Ibid.

12 It is not the place here to engage with Nadine Urbinati's magisterial *Mill on Democracy*, but although she is right to emphasize Mill's 'intoxication with Greece' and desire to apply the political lessons of Athens, I cannot agree that he was not concerned with the problem of how to resolve *institutionally* and in the *practices* of representation – the very title of his book – the dilemma of how to secure popular consent and good government simultaneously. As a close reader of Plato, Grote and de Tocqueville, among others, it was impossible for him not to be concerned with that burning question; and his words prove it.

13 C. S. Emden, *The People and the Constitution* (1956), p. 201.

14 John Stuart Mill, *Considerations on Representative Government* (1861), Chapter 3.

15 Ibid.
16 Op. cit., Chapter 5.
17 Ibid.
18 Op. cit., Chapter 1.
19 Op. cit., Chapter 6.
20 Ibid.
21 Op. cit., Chapter 7.
22 Ibid.
23 Op. cit., Chapter 8.
24 Ibid.
25 Ibid.
26 Ibid.
27 Ibid.
28 Ibid.
29 My colleague Dr Callum Barrell draws my attention to the fact that Mill accepted that his idea of plural voting, which he first put forward in his 'Thoughts on Parliamentary Reform' of 1859, was 'obnoxious' to democratic sentiment, but that in the absence of other ways of coupling a universal franchise with good government he would continue to propose it not as 'an immediately practical measure but as a standard of theoretic excellence'.
30 Mill, op. cit., Chapter 5.

7 Alternative Democracies and Anti-democracies

1   R. Liogier, *New York Times*, syndicated 14 April 2017.
2   Carole Pateman, *Participation and Democratic Theory* (1970), p. 4.
3   Joseph Schumpeter, *Capitalism, Socialism and Democracy* (1943).
4   Schumpeter, op. cit., pp. 256–8.
5   Ibid, p. 269.
6   The debate can be found online at: http://www.learnliberty.org/blog/is-democracy-overrated.
7   Ibid.
8   Ibid.
9   http://www.learnliberty.org/blog/is-democracy-overrated-no.
10 http://www.learnliberty.org/blog/is-democracy-overrated.
11 http://www.learnliberty.org/blog/is-democracy-overrated-no.
12 Ibid.
13 Ibid.
14 Thucydides, *The Peloponnesian War*, Chapter 17.

8 Why It Has Gone Wrong

1 Lord Hailsham, 'Elective Dictatorship', *The Listener*, 21 October 1976, p. 496.
2 Vindu Goel and Eric Lichtblau (*New York Times*), 'Russian agents behind Yahoo breach, US says', *Boston Globe*, March 15, 2017.
3 Sam Levin, 'Pay to Sway', *Guardian*, 13 June 2017.
4 Carole Cadwalladr, 'Revealed: how US billionaire helped to back Brexit', *Observer*, 25 February 2017.
5 Justin Hendrix and David Carroll, 'Confronting a Nightmare for Democracy: Personal Data, Personalized Media and Weaponized Propaganda' (4 May 2017) medium.com/@profcarroll/confronting-a-nightmare-for-democracy-5333181ca675.
6 Daniel Kahneman, *Thinking Fast and Slow* (2011).
7 See Appendix I for an analysis of the motivations behind the campaign to remove the UK from the EU.
8 Carole Cadwalladr, '"Dark money"' is threat to integrity of UK elections, say leading academics', *Observer*, 1 April 2017.
9 Ibid.

9 Making Representative Government Work

1 Edmund Burke, Speech to the Electors of Bristol (3 November 1774), *Works 1*, pp. 446–8.
2 Benjamin Constant, *The Liberty of the Ancients Compared with that of the Moderns*.
3 Quentin Skinner, *Liberty Before Liberalism* (1988).
4 I think a fourth conception of liberty resolves the conflict between the Hobbesian 'lack of restraint' view and the Skinnerian or republican view that the mere existence of authority, or what he calls 'domination' (even if never exercised), negates liberty. Consider the first and third person perspectives in this. From the first person perspective the distinction between complete and permanent lack of restraint on one's choices and actions from an authority which exists, and life under no form of authority, would be a distinction without a difference. From a third person perspective, the requirement that there can be no true liberty unless there is no domination is something of a No True Scotsman argument. For suppose, as the social contract theorists

indeed did, that the authority in question is constituted by agreement for the valid purposes that the social-contractarians specified, but that there are inalienable freedoms (to life, property and liberty of the person, as Locke had it), then the existence of the thus-constituted authority or dominion does not negate what the constituters reserved from interference or restraint. As Isaiah Berlin argued, it is hard to make sense of *lack* of freedom in the absence of interference with it, nor freedom without immunity from such interference. The thought that anarchy might make for 'true' freedom prompts an interesting reflection: in such a state of affairs one would probably be vastly less free than under a system of active government in which individuals are protected from the depredations of stronger and greedier individuals and groups.

5 This example exactly parallels, in numbers and outcome, the Brexit vote in the 2016 UK referendum on EU membership.

10 The People and the Constitution

1 In recent referenda of significance in Britain there has been no consistency in the observance of these requirements, which are the least that common sense requires. In the 1979 Scottish devolution referendum a minimum majority of 40% of the total electorate was stipulated; although 51% of those who voted on the day voted for devolution, they represented only 32% of the turnout, and devolution was therefore denied. In the Scottish independence referendum of 2014 the franchise was extended beyond the usual general election franchise to include sixteen and seventeen year olds and EU citizens living, working and paying their taxes there. The inclusion of both groups was well justified. Whether or not Scotland was to be independent would have a long-term impact on the young, and they deserved their say therefore. EU citizens paying their taxes there could legitimately invoke the principle that there should be no taxation without representation. There was, however, no supermajority threshold for the change; a simple majority decided the issue.

In the UK's referendum on EU membership in June 2016 neither a franchise ensuring participation of all with a material interest in the outcome, nor a threshold, was specified, because both in the briefing document for MPs beforehand and in the House of Commons debate on the assurance of the Minister for Europe, the referendum was to be advisory only, not binding on either government or Parliament. So the referendum was run on a normal general election franchise with a simple majority rule. There had been debate about extending the franchise, and questions were raised about a threshold; but because the referendum was expressly said to be advisory only, these safeguards were not built in. In the event, and with astonishing lack of questioning, the government treated the outcome – a 51.9% vote to leave the EU, representing 37% of the restricted franchise on the turnout – as binding and sufficient.

2 To be precise, the first parliament summoned in England was in 1254, when Queen Eleanor, acting as regent for Henry III while he was in France, and on his instruction, summoned a parliament to raise money needed by Henry. The parliament of 1254 consisted of knights of the shires; de Montfort's parliament consisted of two representatives from each shire and two from each chartered town.

3 C. S. Emden, *The People and the Constitution*, p. 317. The authority he is referring to is A. F. Pollard, *The Evolution of Parliament* (1926).

4 Burke, op. cit., p. 318.

5 Brougham in A. Aspinall, *Lord Brougham and the Whig Party* (2005), pp. 318–19.

6 Ibid., p. 317.

Conclusion

1 Members of the Electoral College are in principle free to make their own judgment about whom to appoint to the White House, and if their judgment differs from that of voters, they are known as 'faithless electors' – and are entitled to be so.

2 Martin Gilens and Benjamin L. Page, 'Testing Theories of American Politics: Elites, Interest Groups, and Average Citizens', *Perspectives on Politics*, Volume 12, Issue 3, September 2014, pp. 564–81.

3 William G. Howell and Terry M. Moe, *Relic: How the Constitution Undermines Effective Government* (2016).

4 I have argued for these propositions repeatedly and from different angles in a series of articles for the *New European* newspaper between July 2016 and March 2017; the articles are also available online at www.acgrayling.com.

Appendix I: Brexit

1 One of the Brexit proponents, David Davis, says publicly in Department for Exiting the European Union replies to correspondents that the 51.9% referendum majority was 'clear, overwhelming and unarguable'. When the Supreme Court required the government to hold a parliamentary debate about triggering Article 50, and it voted 8-3 – a 73% majority – he said publicly that this majority is 'tenuous'.

Appendix II: Failures of Democracy Elsewhere

1 Francis Fukuyama, *The Origins of Political Order* (2011), p. 5.
2 George Monbiot, *How Did We Get Into This Mess?* (2016), p. 3.

INDEX

References to notes are indicated by n.